HU

DISCOVERY COMMUNICATIONS
Founder, Chairman, and Chief Executive Officer:
  John S. Hendricks
President and Chief Operating Officer:
  Judith A. McHale
President, Discovery Enterprises Worldwide:
  Michela English
Senior Vice President, Discovery Enterprises Worldwide:
  Judy Harris

DISCOVERY PUBLISHING
Vice President, Publishing: Natalie Chapman
Editorial Director: Rita Thievon Mullin
Senior Editor: Mary Kalamaras
Editorial Coordinator: Heather Quinlan

DISCOVERY CHANNEL RETAIL
Product Development: Tracy Fortini
Naturalist: Steve Manning

DISCOVERY COMMUNICATIONS, INC., produces high-quality television programming, interactive media, books, films, and consumer products. DISCOVERY NETWORKS, a division of Discovery Communications, Inc., operates and manages the Discovery Channel, TLC, Animal Planet, the Travel Channel, and the Discovery Health Channel.

Reptiles & Amphibians, An Explore Your World ™ Handbook, was created and produced by ST. REMY MEDIA INC.

Library of Congress Cataloging-in-Publication Data
Discovery Channel reptiles & amphibians: an explore your world handbook.--1st ed.
  p. cm.
  ISBN 1-56331-839-3 (pbk.)
  1. Reptiles. 2. Amphibians. I. Title: Reptiles and amphibians. II. Discovery Channel (Firm).
QI.644.D48   2000
597.9--dc21   99-059155
                                        CIP

Random House website address:
http://www.atrandom.com
Discovery Channel Online website address:
http://www.discovery.com
Printed in the United States of America on acid-free paper
First Edition   10 9 8 7 6 5 4 3 2 1

CONSULTANTS

Robert Hansen, editor of *Herpetological Review,* lives in the Sierra Nevada Mountains of California. He conducts research on amphibians and reptiles of the western United States and Mexico.

F. Wayne King, curator of herpetology at the Florida Museum of Natural History, has advised more than twenty-five countries and government agencies, as well as innumerable organizations and programs, on the conservation of reptiles. Professor King has also published more than 145 scientific, popular, and World Wide Web publications.

David Rodrigue is a wildlife biologist and assistant director of the St. Lawrence Valley Natural History Society's Ecomuseum, a wildlife park devoted to education and conservation in Ste. Anne de Bellevue, Quebec. He also coordinates the atlas of amphibians and reptiles of Quebec and the Quebec amphibian populations' monitoring program, as well as other herpetological research programs. Rodrigue's personal and professional interest in exotic reptiles and amphibians dates back many years.

Andrew D. Walde is an avid naturalist and contract field biologist who has contributed to a wide variety of North American research projects, including topics on habitat restoration, ornithology, mammalogy, and herpetology. He has a Masters of Science degree from McGill University in Montreal, Quebec, where he conducted research on the ecology of the wood turtle.

John Wilkinson is a council member of the British Herpetological Society and international coordinator of the Declining Amphibian Populations Task Force. A lifelong student of amphibian biology and conservation, Wilkinson is also the editor of *Froglog,* a newsletter enabling three thousand amphibian scientists and conservationists worldwide to share their knowledge and concerns.

reptiles &
amphibians

An **EXPLORE
YOUR WORLD**™
Handbook

DISCOVERY BOOKS
New York

Contents

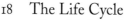

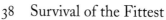

THE WORLD OF REPTILES & AMPHIBIANS

A Herpetologist's Primer

From small, wormlike caecilians to intimidating heavyweights like crocodiles, the variety of living amphibians and reptiles is remarkable. Yet despite their differences, all the species are linked by a common history dating back hundreds of millions of years.

Often unobtrusive and secretive, amphibians and reptiles have long been the subject of myths and legends—and also a source of apprehension and revulsion. While much about these creatures remains shrouded in mystery, even a brief look is enough to make clear that they are more deserving of our fascination than our fear.

The joint study of amphibians and reptiles is called herpetology, from the Greek word *herpo*, meaning to creep or crawl. When this branch of zoology was established in the eighteenth century, scientists didn't distinguish between amphibians and reptiles. It is now evident that these two animal classes have more differences than similarities. As one scientist has observed, reptiles are as distinct from amphibians as fish are from mammals.

Today's world is home to more than twelve thousand amphibian and reptile species (about 70 percent are reptiles). This count exceeds the number of bird or mammal species. The exact figure is a matter of debate because scientists often disagree on how to classify various reptiles and amphibians, and new species continue to be discovered.

There are three main groups of amphibians: frogs, salamanders, and the less familiar caecilians. The word amphibian comes from the Greek words *amphi* and *bios*, meaning "double life." This refers to the way most amphibians begin life as aquatic larvae and later—after metamorphosis—are land-dwelling creatures.

> *"The earth doth like a snake renew/Her winter weeds outworn."*
>
> — Percy Bysshe Shelley
> *Hellas*

No single physical feature or way of life defines all amphibians. Even metamorphosis is not the rule for every species. Some amphibians never leave water, while others spend their entire life on land. Instead, scientists look for a variety of common characteristics, such as skin, skull, ears, and teeth, before categorizing a creature as an amphibian.

Amphibians evolved from fish about 350 million years ago. Fifty million years later—a short time in evolutionary terms—amphibians gave rise to reptiles, which include five groups: turtles and tortoises, snakes, lizards, alligators and crocodiles, and the lizardlike tuataras. Later still, continuing reptilian evolution produced two new classes of animals: mammals and birds.

In addition to a common history, amphibians and reptiles share one dominant trait: Their body temperature fluctuates with the temperature of their environment. To warm their body, these so-called "cold-blooded" creatures require an external heat source, such as direct sunlight or a burrow of sand warmed by the sun. To maintain an optimum body temperature in very hot climates, some reptiles and amphibians are active only at night and keep to the shade

With characteristics that are part reptilian and part fishlike, some amphibians, like the green frog (Rana clamitans melanota) shown above, are equally at home on land and in the water.

during the hottest part of the day. In cold climates, some species hibernate for several months in the winter. A similar period of prolonged inactivity, called estivation, is also practiced by some species in the hottest climates *(pages 54 to 57)*.

With its tough, impermeable skin and its ability to lay eggs that can withstand long, dry spells, reptiles such as the chameleon (Nahaqua sp.) below are well-suited to life on land.

THE SKELETON

Amphibians and reptiles are classified as tetrapods, or four-limbed animals. This may seem strange given that snakes and some lizards and all caecilian species are limbless. However, these species evolved from limbed creatures into their present form. In fact, with some snakes, such as boas and pythons, a close inspection of the exterior reveals tiny vestiges of legs hidden among the scales. Some lizards have only slightly bigger "reduced" legs, indicating that they, too, are probably evolving toward a limbless state.

Similar to fish, birds, and mammals, amphibians and reptiles have a ridged central vertebral column that must be strong enough to support the rest of the skeleton, the muscles, and the internal organs while still allowing for flexibility of movement. Just how much flexibility these animals have varies greatly. Amphibians possess only one neck vertebra, for example. As a result, they have a short neck and limited head movement. Their backbone ranges from ten to two hundred vertebrae in length. In contrast, snakes have as many as four hundred vertebrae.

The varied lifestyles of amphibians and reptiles are reflected in other distinctive body structures. Caecilians, for example, are largely

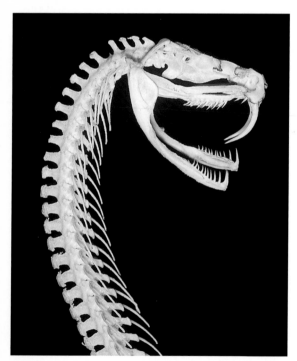

Snakes may be worm-like in appearance, but like all other reptiles and amphibians, they are part of the large grouping, or phylum, known as Chordata—animals that possess a spinal column. Other vertebrates include birds, mammals, and fish.

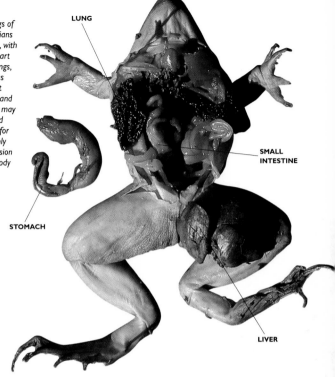

Inside Out

The internal workings of reptiles and amphibians are quite humanlike, with such organs as a heart (not shown here), lungs, and a liver, as well as a digestive tract that includes a stomach and intestines. But there may be some pronounced differences. Snakes, for example, possess only one lung—a concession to their elongated body structure.

LUNG

SMALL INTESTINE

STOMACH

LIVER

subterranean and have a thick, hard skull for more efficient burrowing. Some lizards have one or more weak points between the tail vertebrae of the backbone that allow them to shed their tail, enabling them to escape a predator's grasp. (The tail eventually grows back.) Powerful back legs and an unusually strong vertebral column provide the frog with its spectacular jumping ability. At the other extreme, the tortoise's backbone and ribs are fused to the shell. Only its neck, tail, and legs move freely.

Similar variations are seen in teeth. Some are simple and blunt, others are sharp-edged or feature a broad surface designed for grinding. Many venomous snakes have developed hollow fangs to inject their prey with poison. Certain frogs have no teeth on the lower jaw, while others are toothless on the upper jaw. As they age, most reptiles lose old teeth, with new ones growing in. For their part, living turtles have no teeth at all, but instead have tough ridges along the upper and lower jaws. Turtle fossils from the Triassic period have small teeth on the palate.

Among many reptiles and amphibians, sight, hearing, and smell are the most important senses. Reptiles, except for adult crocodiles and alligators, also rely on their Jacobson's organ—sacs in the roof of the animals' mouth that can "read" airborne chemical cues gathered by the tip of their flicking tongue. Snakes' eyes are protected from dirt and scratches by transparent disks, called brilles, which are shed at the same time as the skin.

SKIN

The function and appearance of the skin are two of the most significant differences between amphibians and reptiles. Amphibians have thin skin—ranging in texture from smooth to rough—that is covered in glands to keep it moist. The requirement of moistness limits many amphibians to humid environments.

Reptile skin is thicker, virtually impervious to water loss, and has a hard, scaly outer layer. Pieces of bone grow in the skin of crocodilians and some lizards, adding strength to this armorlike covering. Unlike the skin of amphibians, the reptiles' outer cover has no respiratory function. The animals take in oxygen, just as humans do, solely through their lungs.

In most adult reptiles, the skin cells flatten and die as they are pushed outward, and several times each year adults shed the external sheath. For snakes, lizards and tuataras, the process includes a resting phase when the cells stop growing temporarily after the outer layer is shed.

Many reptiles and amphibians can lighten or darken their skin depending on their needs. They do it by concentrating or dispersing granules of black pigment, known as melanin, in their skin. This ability enables some animals to blend in better with their background. It also enables reptiles and amphibians to control how their skin absorbs radiation: The darker the skin is, the more heat it absorbs—and vice versa. For creatures that cannot rely on their metabolism to keep their body temperature at optimal levels, altering skin color is an important tool in their thermoregulatory arsenal.

SENSE ORGANS

Depending on the species, the senses show varying degrees of acuteness. Many frogs and lizards, for example, have keen eyesight, which is crucial for their precise tongue-flicking technique of catching prey *(page 46)*, while some lizards attract mates and fend off rival males with a display of gaudy colors.

Caecilians have the least developed senses of all amphibians and reptiles. Living in an underground world of darkness, caecilians do not have to rely on vision or good hearing. Instead, they possess a small tentacle that extends from the eye socket and serves as a smell or touch mechanism to help locate food, predators, or mates.

Hearing is important to the courtship and mating rituals of crocodiles, frogs and toads, and some geckos. Frogs and toads, in particular, have well-developed voices, put to cacaphonous use on summer nights. But many reptiles and amphibians lack a tympanum, or eardrum, or have one covered by skin. Snakes have an earbone that is attached to the jaw, which allows them to detect only low-frequency sounds. Rattlesnakes are deaf to their own rattle.

Aquatic larvae and water-dwelling amphibians interpret their surroundings with so-called lateral-line sense organs, or plaques. These look like dashes or dots and are located along the side of the head and body, enabling the animals to respond to even the slightest movements in water.

Like cats, alligators and crocodiles have a tapetum at the back of each eye—a reflective layer that sends light waves back through the retina a second time, thus improving night vision.

13

Learning to Crawl

Just why amphibians evolved from fish about 350 million years ago is a matter of some disagreement. Many scientists believe that aquatic creatures left the water, for very short periods at first, either to escape from predators or to move from pools that were drying up to ones containing more water. As they spent increasingly longer periods on land, amphibians underwent many dramatic physical changes, such as developing lungs and a body structure that could support the weight of the body in their new home.

Some members of the group, in particular Panderichthyidae, which is believed to have lived 365 million years ago, also had a compressed body similar to that of early amphibians, and lacked dorsal and anal fins. *Crossopterygii* possessed lungs, and some of them had internal nostril openings, called nares, that allowed air intake even with the mouth closed—an important transformation to a life dependent on breathing air.

Along with the similarities, there were also crucial differences

Between Land and Water
Possessing lungs as well as gills, and fins that served as rudimentary legs, the lobe-finned fish (Crossopterygii) was able to make the transformation from life in water to one on land about 350 million years ago.

AMPHIBIAN ADAPTATIONS

The fish most often credited as the common ancestor to all amphibian species belonged to a group of lobe-finned fishes called *Crossopterygii*. These fish had three pairs of fins that were supported by muscles and bony elements rather than by the weaker cartilagenous rays found in other fins. This crucial trait apparently allowed them to move about on land for short distances.

between *Crossopterygii* and even the earliest amphibians, including the organization of the bony elements inside the fins or limbs. In *Crossopterygii*, the ends of these appendages were organized like fins, while even in early amphibians they served more like hands and feet. The enlarged vertebrae where limbs attached to the body presumably enabled the appendages to support the body's weight out of the water.

In *Crossopterygii*, as in other fish, the bones of the skull and the pectoral, or shoulder, girdle were fused together, making it impossible to move the head independently of the body. But in the earliest amphibians, the skull and the pectoral girdle were separated by a functional neck. Other changes in the shape of the head may be related to the different requirements of breathing and feeding on land. Fish usually feed by the suction method, creating sudden negative pressure inside their mouth that draws in food. As land animals, amphibians normally seize their food with their jaws or tongue.

The extinct amphibian Seymouria balerensis broili *lived in the later Permian era, more than 250 million years ago.* Seymouria *was part of a group of animals similar to reptiles that lived at least part of their life on land.*

After the appearance of the first amphibians, a huge variety of forms quickly evolved, including species such as *Mastodonosaurus*, which grew up to sixteen feet (4.9 m) long.

The details of how amphibians developed the new sensory systems and modes of living required for survival on land are not fully understood because there is a gap of about thirty million years in the fossil record. When the next amphibians in that record appeared, many of the adaptations had already occurred.

FROM AMPHIBIANS TO REPTILES

Some fifty million years after the transition from water to land was made, reptiles evolved from amphibians. A major difference between reptiles and amphibians is in the type of eggs they lay. Amphibians lay jelly-covered eggs in water or moist areas. Reptiles produce eggs with tough, dry shells, suitable to a wide range of environments *(pages 18 to 19)*. Before the end of the age of reptiles 65 million years ago, a kind of planetary conquest had occurred: Flying reptiles such as *Pterodactylus* took to the air; some, such as *Stenopterygius* and *Plesiosaurus* returned to the water; and reptiles large and small, both carnivorous and herbivorous, roamed the Earth.

The first known reptiles, found in fossils that date back about 315 million years, differ from amphibians in skull shape and jaw structure. These were probably adaptations for crushing the shells of the insects they ate. As the reptilian diet came to include other reptiles, the group developed more strongly anchored teeth, adaptations to the wrists for grasping prey with both hands, and additional skeletal changes.

The Golden Age of Reptiles

A predecessor of the more famous Tyrannosaurus rex, Acrosanthorsaurus *was a thirteen-foot (4-m) -tall meat-eater that lived 110 million years ago in the southern United States.*

The first dinosaur fossils—teeth and some bones of a thirty-foot (9.1-m) -tall behemoth called Iguanodon—were unearthed in a forest in southern England in the 1820s. Since then, more than five hundred species of the "terrible lizards" have been identified, and scientists suggest that seven hundred to nine hundred still remain to be discovered. While much is known about these extraordinary animals, key mysteries remain, including their sudden disappearance after ruling the Earth for 160 million years, from 225 million to 65 million years ago.

THE FOSSIL RECORD

Dinosaurs were extremely diverse. The formidable carnivore *Tyrannosaurus rex* stood eighteen feet (5.5 m) tall on its back legs, measured about fifty feet (15.2 m) long from tip to tail,

and weighed six tons. Such bulk meant that it was unlikely that *Tyrannosaurus* moved with much speed. Fossilized tracks suggest that the animal stalked prey such as *Brachiosaurus*, a herbivore of astonishing proportions: forty feet (12.2 m) high weighing about seventy tons. Paleontologists believe that such large plant-eaters may have moved in herds in order to increase their chances of survival.

Toward the other end of the scale were small, swift carnivores such as the *Velociraptor*, which measured about six feet (1.8 m) in length (including the tail). Armed with a retractable claw on each back foot and capable of grasping prey with both clawed hands, this small but deadly biped is believed to have hunted in packs, and may have preyed even on the large herbivores. At one fossil site, some bones of a *Tenontosaurus*, a herbivore weighing about eight hundred pounds (363 kg), were found along with several *Deinonychus* specimens (a slightly larger cousin of *Velociraptor*). Presumably, the *Tenontosaurus* was attacked by a pack of *Deinonychus*, several of which died in the fight.

As well as ruling the land, reptiles also took to the air during this period. Close to one hundred species of flying pterosaurs (not in fact dinosaurs, but a separate reptile group) have been identified, including a fish-eating giant called *Pteranodon*, which boasted a twenty-four-foot (7.3-m) wingspan. Fossil evidence now suggests even bigger species of pterosaurs existed as well.

It was long accepted that dinosaurs, like other reptiles, were cold-blooded, or ectothermic. However, some researchers now suggest that in fact at least some were warm-blooded and may have had hairy coats or feathers. The apparently fast-moving, pack-hunting dinosaurs, such as *Velociraptor*, are cited as evidence, because cold-bloodedness is generally associated with much lower levels of activity. This possibility is linked to another increasingly accepted theory that birds are in fact direct descendants of dinosaurs.

AN UNTIMELY END

The abrupt disappearance of dinosaurs has long intrigued scientists. What could have happened to eliminate a group of animals that had adapted to so many different roles over such a long time?

While many theories have been advanced, the most widely held suggests that a cataclysmic event—possibly a meteorite striking the Earth and sending a thick layer of dust into the air—created a dramatically colder climate. Dinosaurs that had adapted very well to warmer conditions may not have been able to adapt fast enough to these new conditions. These same changes may also have altered the vegetation in many areas, resulting in diminished food availability.

However, even this theory doesn't fully explain why many other creatures that lived in the same habitats as dinosaurs managed to survive. Some researchers speculate that animals such as crocodiles and turtles may have been less affected because they are largely aquatic creatures and water moderates the effect of temperature changes. Nonetheless, with the disappearance of dinosaurs and other giant reptiles, mammals became more diverse and successful, taking over as the most prominent vertebrates on the planet.

A park service worker at Dinosaur National Monument in Colorado chips away rocks from a dinosaur bone. Very few skeletons are found intact, so paleontologists usually have to carry out a painstaking reconstruction process.

THE LIFE CYCLE

Amphibians and reptiles, like all living things, are governed by nature's immutable laws: They're born, they live, they die. But within these life stages lie fascinating differences— even among closely related species.

There are fundamental differences between the life cycles of an amphibian and a reptile. Nowhere is this more apparent than during the earliest stages of development. While some reptiles and amphibians, such as many snakes and lizards, give birth to live young, most lay eggs (a process called oviparity). But it is the *type* of eggs they lay that sets reptiles and amphibians so clearly apart.

Amphibian eggs have no shell. Instead, the ova are usually surrounded by one or more dense, gelatinous "envelopes" that provide some protection against predators, pathogens, and other damaging agents. However, the permeable nature of the eggs leaves them vulnerable to their environment. Unless they are kept moist by their surroundings, amphibian eggs will dry out and die.

Reptile eggs, on the other hand, have a protective outer shell—in some instances, soft and leathery, in others, as hard as birds' eggs. Whatever its outer texture, the reptile egg is a self-contained system that protects the embryo from water loss while still allowing it to breathe and develop on dry land.

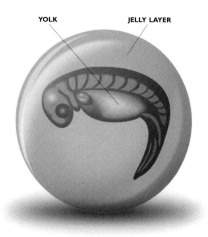

YOLK   JELLY LAYER

Anatomy of an Amphibian Egg
Compared to the reptile egg, the amphibian egg is a simpler affair, with a yolk sac surrounded by one or more jelly layers. Because it lacks a protective outer shell, the amphibian egg must be kept moist, limiting where it can be laid.

The level and type of development that goes on inside the egg varies, too. Nourished by the yolk contained within the egg, most amphibians develop into aquatic, gill-bearing larvae (such as tadpoles, in the case of frogs and toads) before they hatch. Not until the next stage, metamorphosis, do these amphibians become airbreathing, mostly terrestrial adults. Exceptions include most salamander species, which in fact bypass the aquatic larval stage, the eggs hatching instead into miniature versions of the adult. In contrast, all reptile species are fully formed when they hatch.

> *"The turtle lives 'twixt plated decks/Which practically conceal its sex./I think it clever of the turtle/In such a fix to be so fertile."*
>
> — OGDEN NASH

EGG-LAYING VERSUS LIVE BIRTH
Each method of bringing young into the world—egg-laying and live-bearing—has advantages and drawbacks. By laying eggs, known as oviparity, the pregnant female experiences a shorter gestation period and therefore spends less time burdened by her young. On the other hand, eggs are highly susceptible to being eaten by predators and most live young can take care of themselves from the moment they're born. Eggs may also be subjected to temperatures that are too hot or too cold, while a viviparous female regulates the temperature of her unborn progeny as she regulates her own.

Live-bearing appears to have developed in response to specific environmental conditions. For example, in northern and mountainous regions, where the cold weather might hinder eggs from developing outside the mother's body, the incidence of live-bearing increases significantly.

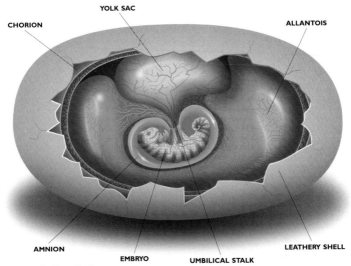

Anatomy of a Reptile Egg
Inside the reptile's protective, permeable shell, the embryo is encased by three fluid-filled sacs: the chorion, the allantois, and the amnion. The allantois and the chorion both contain blood vessels that direct the exchange of oxygen through the egg shell. The allantois also collects the embryo's waste products. For its part, the amnion forms a closed sac around the embryo that acts as an additional layer of protection against dehydration and disturbance. The yolk sac provides food energy in the form of fat and protein.

Courtship & Mating

Amphibians and reptiles court and mate in a myriad of ways, from the chorus of male frogs and head butting of iguanas to the tale lashing of salamanders and the underwater embrace of turtles.

In a mating embrace known as amplexus, the male tree frog (Hyla ebraccata) grabs the female behind her front legs. The position places the reproductive organs of the two close together so that sperm can be spread over the eggs as they are laid.

Amphibian courtship occurs mostly in or around water. Often the suitors will travel considerable distances—up to several miles—to the water where they hatched and developed. Once in their native pond, some males, such as bullfrogs (*Rana catesbeiana*), diligently guard watery territories up to twenty feet (6 m) in diameter. Like miniature sumo wrestlers, they may grapple fiercely with rival males for territorial control. Most frogs have balloonlike vocal sacs, either one large sac in the chin area or one on each side of the throat. The sacs act as resonating chambers as they fill with air that then passes through the vocal cords *(pages 58 to 59)*.

Selecting a mate by the quality of his territory, a female bullfrog slowly swims close to her chosen suitor and makes the selection final by touching him with her leg or nose. Then, he wraps his front legs around her upper body, holding her tightly in a mating embrace, called amplexus, that can last several hours in some species. As she lays masses of eggs— up to twenty thousand—he emits sperm to fertilize them.

With little hope of setting up and defending territories, smaller bullfrogs may wait at the edge of territories in hopes of intercepting females attracted by the larger

Maleless Reproduction

With some lizards and at least one snake, young are born from eggs unfertilized by males. The reason? There are no males. Also known as "virgin birth," parthenogenesis is usually the result of the hybridization of two species. The offspring of these all-female species are genetically identical. Such reproduction has an advantage: Favorable traits created by mutations can be passed along more quickly from generation to generation. But since the gene pool among these species is more limited, they are less able to respond quickly and alter their genetic makeup when abrupt changes in the environment demand it.

frogs. These satellite males are usually displaced during mating attempts by larger frogs, but their strategy still gives them an opportunity to mate without singing or defending territories, both of which are energy-draining activities.

While most frogs use vocalization to attract a mate, mating in salamanders is often a silent affair. Many salamanders, like frogs, have a courtship embrace, with the male gradually enticing the female to be receptive. In some aquatic species, the male attracts a female by lashing his tail back and forth, fanning secretions from his reproductive gland toward her. He later deposits a sperm package, called a spermatophore, then guides the female over it by nudging or leading her or clasping her head. She then picks up the sperm package in her cloaca (genital opening).

To encourage the female to accept his advances, the male mountain dusky salamander (*Desmognathus ochrophaeus*) rasps the female's skin with his teeth, inoculating her with a chemical from his chin gland.

Without the help of sound to attract a mate, some male salamanders congregate to attract attention. The male red-spotted newt (*Notophthalmus viridescens*) competes for approaching females, with the strongest male continuing the courtship. Male and female sink to the bottom, with the male circling the female in a sort of dance, each rising to the surface occasionally for a gulp of air. In a form of amplexus, the male swims about transporting the female.

AMONG THE REPTILES

By laying their eggs on land, reptiles have freed themselves from the requirement that draws most amphibians back to water for courting. Many depend on visual signals to attract a mate. Male lizards, for example, are often brightly colored. They are the ones that initiate courtship, but they can only progress with mating if their prospective partner signals that she is receptive. The male green anole (*Anolis carolinensis*) bobs his head, expanding a colorful fold of skin, known as a dewlap, that hangs from the throat to advertise his

A male Cuban anole (Anolis equestris) displays his dewlap extension, seeking to attract prospective mates and ward off would-be rivals.

mating intentions and also to warn away competing males. He often will approach a female with a stiff-legged walk. If she is receptive, she will arch her back and the male will sidle up beside her, biting her neck and clasping the base of her tail with his hind limbs prior to mating.

At the beginning of the mating season, male Bengal monitor lizards (*Varanus bengalensis*) wrestle, rearing up on hindlegs and grappling. The weaker one usually gives up before it is injured. Male marine iguanas (*Amblyrhynchus cristatus*) compete for territories by engaging in head-butting contests, quickly whirling to bite a rival at the base of its tail. When approaching a female, a male komodo dragon (*Varanus komodoensis*), the world's largest lizard, presses his snout against the female's body, flicking constantly with his tongue to gain chemical cues about her receptiveness. He scratches her back with his long claws and may also make a ratchetlike noise. If she is unreceptive, she rises, inflates her neck, and hisses loudly. Otherwise, the male crawls onto the female's back and flicks his tongue on her head while rubbing the base of her tail with his hindlegs.

SNAKES, TURTLES, AND ALLIGATORS

During mating season, female snakes emit a chemical scent, or pheromone, from their cloaca as they slither about on the ground. A male that picks up the scent by tongue-flicking will immediately change course and follow the scent trail in an effort to catch up to the female. Approaching her slowly, he stimulates her by rubbing his chin on her back, wrapping around her body

In some species of lizards and snakes, such as the southern alligator lizards (Elgaria multicarinate) shown here, the male grabs the female's neck to hold her in place during mating.

as he slowly works his way forward until his chin is on the back of her neck. When the female is ready, she slightly raises the rear part of her body, exposing her genital opening.

Mating in colder climates often occurs just after snakes emerge from hibernation. Occasionally, snakes such as the red-sided garter (*Thamnophis sirtalis parietalis*) may hibernate in groups numbering in the thousands *(pages 30 to 31)*. Males emerge from hibernation first and mass together as they wait for females. Sometimes a single female that emerges afterward is surrounded by mating balls of up to a hundred or more males intertwined in a writhing mass. In some species, after a male has finished mating, he may leave a kind of plug in the female's cloaca that stops other males from mating. Some males are also female mimics, producing the courtship pheromone that confuses their rivals while they go off in search of a real female.

Courtship among turtles can be a simple affair. A male painted turtle (*Chrysemys picta*) will swim around a female in circles. While facing her, he strokes her head and neck with his long claws. If willing, she touches him and they sink to the bottom where they mate, the male holding her tightly with his long claws. Mating in the water helps neutrally buoyant turtles maintain their bal-

Mating for the eastern box turtle (Terrapene carolina) demands that the male stand on his back legs and grab the female's shell with his hind feet, tipping beyond the vertical to copulate.

ance. But on land, it seems an impossible dream for a male to precariously balance on a female's shell during the mating process. Large land turtles, such as the Galapagos tortoise (*Geochelone elephantopus*), have an ingenious solution to this problem. The underside of the shell, or plastron, of the male is curved inward in a concave shape. This fits perfectly onto the convex, or rounded, shape of the top of the female's shell.

The primeval, thunderlike roar of a male American alligator (*Alligator mississippiensis*) serves to attract a mate and warn other males away. Females seem to take the initiative in courting. Having approached the males and chosen a suitor, a female may wait for several days before mating. With the pair lying side by side, the female arches her tail upward; the male responds by lifting his tail and copulating with her for several minutes.

The Wonder of Metamorphosis

Most amphibians spend a short time as aquatic larvae, then undergo metamorphosis—an often abrupt and dramatic transformation into adulthood. Amphibians are the only vertebrates to experience this unusual growth spurt. No reptiles have such a life stage.

Life Begins
A few days into life, a tadpole's gills take on a feather-like appearance and begin to work. Soon the tadpole starts to swim freely and feed on tiny plant particles.

Of all amphibians, frogs and toads undergo the most remarkable changes during metamorphosis. Tadpoles, as larval frogs and toads are familiarly known, live entirely in the water, breathing through gills and propelling their round, legless bodies with a long tail. They differ so much from adult frogs and toads that they could be mistaken for completely unrelated creatures. The larvae of one frog species—the appropriately named paradoxical frog (*Pseudis paradoxa*), found in South America—not only looks nothing like the adult, but is as much as four times bigger.

Identity Crisis
Six to eight weeks after hatching, the tadpole is no longer a tadpole, but not yet a frog or a toad. A sleeker body and hindlegs allow more aggressive swimming.

The change from newly hatched larva to young adult varies considerably from species to species, but is twelve to sixteen weeks for most frog and toad species. The process involves a series of striking developments and intermediary stages. About a week into life, internal gills develop and a membrane grows over the tadpole's external gills. Soon hindlegs begin to sprout from tiny buds, the body grows longer, and the head becomes more distinct. Roughly nine weeks after the tadpole hatches, its front legs spring—

Coming into Focus
After about eight to ten weeks, with all four limbs in evidence and eyes and mouth more prominent, the tadpole looks much like a small frog with a very long tail.

elbow-first—from the chamber housing the gills. With the gradual switch from a herbivorous to a carnivorous diet, the adult digestive tract is reduced to as little as 15 percent of its original length. Over the last few weeks of development, the tail shrinks, absorbed by the body for nourishment, and eventually disappears completely. The final result is a perfectly formed, tiny frog or toad that is ready to hop from the water and begin anew on four feet.

Metamorphosis is triggered by hormones produced in the pituitary and thyroid glands, and it is further influenced by environmental factors such as water and air temperature. Low temperatures, for example, can inhibit the release of thyroxine, a hormone contributed by the thyroid gland. As a result, metamorphosis is delayed and tadpoles remain in their larval state for a full year, or even two, until the temperature once again favors development.

Looking to the Land
Over the next few weeks, the body reabsorbs the tail. Brief visits onto land begin.

In most salamanders and caecilians, metamorphosis produces minor changes since the larvae of these creatures already resemble smaller versions of adults. These modifications include resorption of the tail fin, loss of the gills, and development of lungs. Changes to the digestive tract are minimal since salamanders are actively carnivorous in the larval and adult stages.

ARRESTED DEVELOPMENT
Not all salamanders develop into fully formed adults that live on land. Often metamorphosis appears to stall, leaving individuals with juvenile characteristics—such as external gills or the absence of eyelids—yet also with the capacity to reproduce. This phenomenon is called paedomorphosis and allows a continuation of the aquatic stage. In some cases,

paedomorphosis occurs when the aquatic habitats of larvae are more hospitable than the terrestrial habitats available to adults. After all, why leave a comfortable existence in the water if life on the land holds little promise?

Sometimes paedomorphosis is a temporary response to environmental conditions. The Mexican axolotl (*Ambystoma mexicanum*), for example, retains its gills when insufficient iodine levels in the environment halt production of a hormone required to complete metamorphosis. In other species, such as the mudpuppy (*Necturus maculosus*) of eastern North America and the olm (*Proteus anguinus*) of Yugoslavia and northern Italy, paedomorphosis has evolved into a fixed genetic trait: These salamanders spend their entire life in the water.

All Grown Up
As frogs reach adult size, the tail disappears or is reduced to nothing more than a stump. Some frogs reach a mature breeding stage in as little as a year, while most aquatic frogs reach maturity after about four years.

Caring for Their Young

The female reticulated poison-dart frog (Dendrobates reticulatus) transports tadpoles on her back to new sources of water. The young are kept in place during the journey by a sticky mucous covering on the mother's skin.

Compared to mammals and birds, reptiles and amphibians might seem like neglectful parents. Many of them—turtles, lizards, snakes, and some frogs—don't care for their young at all: They choose a good site and they might build a nest, but once they've laid their eggs, they leave. But there are numerous exceptions to this practice. Some species guard their eggs until they hatch. Others provide food for their offspring. And crocodiles and alligators, the most doting parents of all, continue to care for their young until they are up to two years old.

GUARDING THE EGGS

Staying with the eggs is the simplest form of parental care. Eggs have certain physical needs that a guarding adult can meet. Many amphibians lay their eggs on land, and the eggs must be kept from drying out. Some adult salamanders coil around their eggs and raise them off the ground when the soil is parched. The flaming poison-arrow frog (*Dendrobates pumilio*) has another technique: The male, which guards the eggs, releases water stored in his bladder to keep them moist.

For eggs laid in the water there is little risk of drying out, but a few species do attend aquatic eggs. The male or female olm (*Proteus anguinus*) that stays with the eggs waves its tail to change the water currents near them. The African tree toad (*Nectophryne afra*) does the same thing

by kicking its feet in the water. Scientists are not entirely sure why these aquatic parents feel compelled to agitate the water in these ways. It might be to increase the amount of oxygen available to the eggs, ensuing better embryo development.

Eggs also may need warmth, which a guarding adult can provide. Some female snakes, such as the carpet python (*Morelia spilota*) of Australia, will leave their eggs to warm themselves by basking in the sun, then curl around the eggs again. The Indian python (*Python molurus*) can raise her own body temperature by contracting and relaxing her muscles. When the temperature falls, she contracts more frequently—up to about thirty times a minute. The result is much like the shivering reflex of mammals, except that in the python's case it is voluntary, enabling her to keep the eggs at a temperature of about eighty-six degrees Fahrenheit (30°C).

Staying with the eggs also means that the adult can protect them

A Full Stomach

The female of the appropriately named gastric brooding frog (*Rheobatrachus silus*) broods her young inside her stomach. The eggs are fertilized and laid, then the female swallows them. They stay in her stomach through all the stages of development and hop out of her mouth as fully developed frogs.

from predators. For some snakes, coiling around the eggs provides camouflage. The male nest-building gladiator frog (*Hyla rosenbergi*) scoops out a shallow, water-filled basin in the soil at the edge of the water and the female deposits the eggs in a film on top of the water. The male then defends the area from other males that might disturb the water, for once the liquid's surface tension is broken, the eggs will sink and die.

Few snakes brood their eggs. Those that give birth to live young, such as the copperhead (Agkistrodon contortrix) shown at left, will abandon their offspring at birth, leaving them to fend for themselves.

FREE RIDE

Some amphibians lay their eggs on land but live in the water as adults, so the young need to get from the site where they begin their life to a pool or stream. Nature may take care of the transportation. For example, the eggs of the marbled salamander (*Ambystoma opacum*) are laid in dried up ponds and are submerged by winter rains. In certain other species, the adults do the job. During the form of amphibian mating known as amplexus, the male midwife toad (*Alytes obstetricans*) wraps the long strands of fertilized eggs around his hindlegs and carries them with him until it is time for them to hatch. Then, he releases them in shallow water.

FULL-SCALE PARENTING

Crocodiles and alligators provide the most extensive parenting among reptiles and amphibians. They not only build nests and guard their eggs, they also help the hatchlings to get out of their shells, carry the young to water, and stay with them for varying lengths of time. The Nile crocodile (*Crocodylus niloticus*) buries her eggs in a nest she digs with her hindlegs and stays nearby until they're ready to hatch. When the

Who Cares?

Paternal involvement in caring for eggs or young is higher among amphibians that fertilize their eggs externally than in species that fertilize internally. In some species, the male simply guards the eggs. Others take a more active role. The male of various species of poison-arrow frogs carries the tadpoles on his back from the terrestrial hatching site to water, where they will complete their development. And the male Darwin frog (*Rhinoderma darwinii*) shown above collects the fertilized eggs one by one with his mouth and holds them in his vocal sacs until they are fully metamorphosed into froglets, at which point they hop out.

Both male and female alligators provide care to their young, carrying them to water in their mouth or allowing them to bask in the sunshine on their back.

young call to her from their eggs, she excavates them from the nest, gently breaking any unopened eggs to help the babies emerge. Then, she collects them all in her mouth and carries them to the water, where they are released. The hatchlings will remain with the female and male for about six to eight weeks. Both parents will defend the young during this time, and even other adult crocodiles will respond to the distress calls of any hatchlings.

The American alligator (*Alligator mississippiensis*) is even more solicitous of her young, keeping the nest where she laid the eggs properly moist by lying on it after she leaves the water, and protecting them when necessary by puffing up her body and lunging at intruders. Once the hatchlings emerge, they may stay with their mother for up to two years.

Making a Spectacle

From herds of zebras and giraffes grazing on the plains of Africa to flocks of Canada geese flying in giant V formations, the group behavior of animals in the wild provides some of the most memorable spectacles in nature. While not always the most social creatures, amphibians and reptiles also occasionally congregate in impressive numbers.

One of the most dramatic examples of group behavior in the reptile world occurs along a ninety-mile (145-km) stretch of coastline in northeastern Mexico. Every year, thousands of migrating Atlantic ridley turtles (*Lepidochelys kempi*) take to the beaches of this region in the course of a single day and dig their nests in the sand. A similar annual invasion of the olive ridley (*Lepidochelys olivacea*) occurs in Costa Rica.

In the past, arriving turtle populations were so dense that spectators on the beach could walk for miles along the back of the shells, never touching the sand. Conveniently for sightseers, the phenomenon happens in broad day-

light. But without the protective cover of darkness, the turtles were a very easy mark for hunters, who slaughtered them in huge numbers. Legislation in Mexico and Costa Rica has stemmed the decline, but Atlantic and olive ridley turtles remain endangered species.

Group behavior in amphibians and reptiles is most often related to migration and reproduction, but other factors can also play a part. Snakes that spend the winter in northern habitats survive the coldest months by hibernating in deep crevices below the frost line. If such sites are hard to come by, hundreds or even thousands of snakes are forced to share the same den. In the spring, the snakes often emerge at the same time, covering the ground in a thick layer of writhing bodies.

Space restrictions and the need to stay warm are also the ingredients in a well-documented reptile spectacle in the Galapagos Islands. Here, large numbers of marine iguanas bask

Marine iguanas (Amblyrhynchus cristatus) in the Galapagos Islands bask near the water. After diving into the ocean and feeding on algae, the iguanas experience a sharp drop in body temperature and must quickly expose their body to sunlight to warm up.

Every year, thousands of female olive ridley turtles (Lepidohelys olivacea) migrate to Nancite Beach in Costa Rica to lay their eggs. The predictable arrival of this and other sea-turtle species have made them easy targets for hunters in the past.

together on rocks along the shore to warm up after feeding in the surrounding cool water. With a limited number of convenient places to stretch out, the males of this lizard species don't bother with aggressive displays of territoriality that might otherwise keep them apart. Instead, males and females crowd together like prehistoric sunbathers on a very rocky Riviera beach.

Banding together can also provide protection against predators because only a small percentage of the group is likely to be snatched up by enemy jaws or beaks while the rest survive. Unfortunately, this is rarely an effective technique against the most dangerous predator of all: humans. As a result, many of the vast conjugations of amphibians and reptiles that were once a feature of the natural world have shared the fate of the tremendous herds of bisons that formerly roamed the Plains. And the unhappy trend continues. Until recently, for example, large rafts of breeding sea snakes could be seen off the coast of the Philippines. One display measured ten feet (3 m) wide by sixty miles (97 km) long. But with huge numbers of the snakes routinely killed for their skin, the snakes have become endangered; and yet another awesome natural spectacle no longer occurs.

Homing & Migration

The world of amphibians and reptiles is often very small. Most species live out their life within a few hundred yards of where they were born. And yet there are species that journey far afield, traveling to the same breeding pond year after year or venturing hundreds—or even thousands—of miles across the ocean to nesting sites they may not have seen in decades.

Amphibians and reptiles vary greatly in their way-finding abilities. Some turtles have trouble finding their way back home when they are moved more than a few hundred yards. By contrast, red-bellied newts (*Taricha rivularis*) have been transported up to seven miles (11 km) from their home stream and still found their way to where they were first captured, traversing hills to complete their trip. For those species that migrate, the journeys can be even more impressive. The kings of reptile and amphibian navigation are the green turtles (*Chelonia mydas*) of South America, which leave the beaches of Brazil and cross more than twenty-eight hundred miles (4,500 km) of the Atlantic Ocean before arriving at their nesting site on the tiny island of Ascension *(opposite)*.

FINDING THEIR WAY

How do these animals find their way around? For short trips, the answer may be fairly simple. Turtles and crocodilians can smell bodies of water several hundred yards away. Acoustic cues may also serve a role, leading female frogs, for example, toward a chorus of male frogs that are ready to mate. Some scientists suggest that visual landmarks—familiar burrows, trees, logs, and rocks—can help guide some reptiles and amphibians to their goal.

For longer journeys, the answer is more complex. The greatest feats of reptile and amphibian travel involve continually altering a course without local cues or landmarks to reach a predetermined destination. As with bird migration, there seems to be no single process at work. Reptiles and amphibians rely on a variety of stimuli, including celestial cues from the moon and sun, polarized light, and even a sensitivity to Earth's magnetic field.

Home Base

When sea turtles emerge from their eggs, they immediately head to the water. Their sea-finding sense seems tied to an ability to detect the brightest area on the horizon, typically the reflection of the sun or moon off the water. But this can produce errors. A group of hatchlings once turned away from the sea and invaded the infield of a baseball game in the Virgin Islands, drawn by the stadium lights.

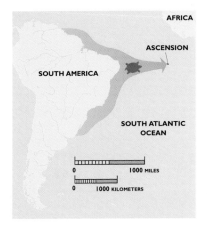

Migration Route of Turtles
The green turtles' voyage from the beaches of Brazil to nesting grounds on tiny Ascension Island in the middle of the Atlantic Ocean seems to involve an awareness of Earth's magnetic field, allowing the turtles to keep on course during a voyage that takes months to complete. Some scientists suggest that the animals' innate "compass" guides them close to their target, at which point smell or visual clues take over to enable the turtles to zero-in on their destination.

Recent research has focused on the role of the light-sensitive pineal gland, which is located on the top of the skull and is connected to the brain. This "third eye" enables some species to perceive polarized light and use it to determine the sun's position. This works even when the animal is blind or the sun is completely obscured by clouds.

The pineal gland may play another role in helping some reptiles and amphibians navigate. Scientists have observed that the red-spotted newt (*Notophthalmus viridescens*) has a sensitivity to Earth's magnetic field that is connected with its pineal gland. By covering the animal's eyes and pineal gland with various combinations of filters, scientists discovered that the newt's perception of the magnetic field depends on an interaction between the particular wavelength of the light that it perceives through its pineal gland—not its eyes—and the geomagnetic field. Other animals that have demonstrated a sensitivity to Earth's magnetic field are alligators and sea turtles. In experiments, loggerhead turtles (*Caretta caretta*), for example, have been observed to change their direction of travel when an artificially created magnetic field is reversed.

The red-bellied newt (Taricha rivularis) can traverse unfamiliar terrain to return to its home. Scientists believe that the animal relies on its sensitivity to the axis of Earth's magnetic field to orient itself during the journey.

33

Growth & Longevity

Most mammals grow continuously until sexual maturity is reached, then stop. But many reptiles and amphibians continue growing throughout their life. One reason for the difference is skeletal structure. Mammalian bones are characterized by an epiphysis, an ossified formation at the end of the bone, separated from the rest of the bone by cartilage. Once growth is complete, the epiphysis fuses with the main part of the bone and no further growth is possible. But the skeletons of reptiles and amphibians typically lack such epiphyses; their bones can continue to get bigger by the process of adding one layer of bone on top of another. Another difference: Since they do not need to maintain their body at a precise temperature, reptiles and amphibians have much lower metabolisms than birds and mammals. This enables them to conserve energy or redirect its use when necessary. During favorable conditions— when food is in good supply and moderate temperatures prevail— reptiles and amphibians can store excess energy as fat. Then, when conditions deteriorate, they can suspend growth, using the available energy to maintain basic body functions. They can restart growth once conditions improve.

Experiments looking at detailed annual energy budgets in some turtles and snakes have shown that most of the energies used from birth to sexual maturity

A New Skin

Unlike mammals and birds, reptiles and amphibians do not slough off the outer layer of their skin continuously, but instead shed it in one big piece or many smaller ones as it needs to be replaced or becomes too small. During the process, also known as ecdysis, the outer layer of the epidermis is separated from the forming replacement layer of skin by mucous secretions, which dry out before the actual shedding occurs. Snakes literally crawl out of their old skin from the nose to the end of the tail, shedding even the transparent scale covering the eye, while an amphibian's skin will split along the mid-dorsal line and slide backward, to be eaten later by the animal. Shedding occurs from every four days for some amphibians to once or twice every year for old, large reptiles.

Anacondas grow up thirty feet (9 m) long. This sixteen-foot (5-m) green anaconda (Eunectes murinus) was captured in Venezuela.

are invested in growth, whereas egg development—or embryo development for live-bearing species—consumes a significant portion of the energy once maturity is reached. Reptiles and amphibians increase by three- to twenty-fold in length and more than one hundred times in mass from the time of birth or hatching to sexual maturity.

GROWING STRONG

Except for some color differences in various species, juvenile reptiles and amphibians are fully functional miniature replicas of their parents. Most grow quickly from birth to sexual maturity, thereby minimizing the time when they are most vulnerable to predators

and environmental changes. For example, members of the genus *Plethodon*, which belong to the lungless salamanders family, accomplish 28 to 33 percent of their total post-hatching growth in their first year, while cane toads (also known as marine, or giant, toads) from South America (*Bufo marinus*) grow from less than a third to a half inch (8 to 12 mm) in length as newly metamorphosed froglets to five inches (120 mm) at six months of age, an increase of more than 1,000 percent.

The little grass frog (Pseudacris ocularis) is one of the world's smallest frogs—barely 0.5 inch (12 mm) long. Primarily nocturnal, it lives from southeastern Virginia to the Florida Keys.

35

A variety of factors affect the rate of growth in reptiles and amphibians, including the genetic potential of an individual, its size at hatching, its efficiency at capturing prey and the energy used in doing so, and the abundance and quality (digestibility and caloric content) of the food available during its juvenile growing period and the length of this period (how early or late maturity typically occurs for a given species). In some species, sexual dimorphism, a size discrepancy between mature males and females, results in a proportionally faster growth for the larger of the two sexes. Temperature also plays a part because it affects the rate of the chemical reactions of growth. When temperatures decrease, metabolism slows and, with it, all cellular processes, which then increase when temperatures become more favorable.

VARYING LIFE SPANS

Longevity in reptiles and amphibians is often related to the reaching of one major event in the life of the animals: sexual maturity. Depending on how early or late it occurs in an animal's life, sexual maturity will affect the number of descendants a reptile or amphibian contributes to its own species. It also plays a key role in determining how long many animals will live.Once sexual maturity is reached, most of the energies of an animal will be directed toward the annual reproductive cycle. This exacts its toll. Generally speaking, species that take a long time to mature live longer and produce smaller numbers of offspring every year than those species that mature more quickly.

Amphibians enter the reproduction phase of their life after periods that range from four to six months for the West African screeching frog

RECORD SIZES AND WEIGHTS FOR REPTILES AND AMPHIBIANS		
SPECIES (SMALLEST, LARGEST)	SIZE	WEIGHT
1) Mexican lungless salamander	1 inch (25 mm)	n/a
Chinese giant salamander	6 feet (1.8 m)	143 lb (65 kg)
2) Brazilian brachycephalid frog	0.5 inch (13 mm)	n/a
African goliath frog	11.75 inches (30 cm)	7.25 lb (3.3 kg)
3) Speckled Cape tortoise	3.25 inches (8.3 cm)	0.3 lb (0.14 kg)
Leatherback turtle	8 feet (2.4 m)	1,890 lb (857 kg)
4) Monito gecko	1.3 inches (3.3 cm)	0.00026 lb (0.00012 kg)
Komodo dragon	10.25 feet (3.1 m)	364 lb (165 kg)
5) Brahminy blind snake	4.4 inches (11.2 cm)	n/a
Green anaconda	33 feet (10 m)	550 lb (249 kg)
Reticulated python	32.3 feet (9.8 m)	Less than anaconda
6) Cuvier's dwarf caiman	5 feet (1.5 m)	n/a
Indo-Pacific saltwater crocodile	23 feet (7 m)	2,200 lb (998 kg)

The Aldabra tortoises (Testudo gigantea) *from the Seychelles Islands are the longest-living reptiles known, surviving more than a century in captivity. Life spans in the wild tend to be shorter.*

(*Arthroleptis poecilonotus*) to seven years for the hellbender salamander (*Cryptobranchus alleganiensis*). To reach sexual maturity, reptiles require from two to four months, as for the lizard *Anolis poecilopus*, to as high as forty to fifty years, as for the green sea turtle (*Chelonia mydas*).

Finding out the number of years a species in the wild lives is difficult work for scientists since reptiles and amphibians can be relatively tough to track. Some mark-recapture studies have provided valuable data, and the advent of radio-telemetry— affixing a transmitter to an animal so its movements can be tracked by antennae or, in some cases, satellites—has yielded a wealth of information. In general, large species of reptiles and amphibians seem to live longer.

How old can the oldest reptiles and amphibians live? An Aldabra tortoise (*Testudo gigantea*) reportedly survived for 152 years after it was captured as an adult in the Indian Ocean's Seychelles Islands. Other examples of long life among captive reptiles and amphibians are 120 years for a European pond turtle (*Emys orbicularis*), seventy-three years for an American alligator (*Alligator mississippiensis*), seventy years for an alligator snapping turtle (*Macroclemys temmincki*), forty-five years for an African ball python (*Python regius*), thirty-three years for a Cayman Island iguana (*Cyclura nubila caymanensis*), and forty years for a Japanese giant salamander (*Andrias japonicus*).

SURVIVAL OF THE FITTEST

Amphibians and reptiles survive in almost every habitat on the planet, even deserts and marshes, mountains and oceans. Their success is testament to the remarkable adaptations each species has developed to cope with the world around it.

It seems fitting that reptiles and amphibians—as early ancestors of the first creatures to walk the Earth—played a key role in kindling Charles Darwin's concept of evolution and survival of the fittest. The nineteenth-century English scientist noted many curious-looking animals in his momentous round-the-world voyage aboard the HMS *Beagle*. The giant Galapagos tortoise (*Geochelone elephantopus*), in particular, caught Darwin's eye: The islands in the Galapagos archipelago feature different subspecies of the giant turtle, each with adaptive traits tailor-made for its environment. Turtles that live on the drier islands, for example, possess longer necks and limbs, which make it easier for them to reach the taller vegetation typically found there.

From the Namib desert of Africa to the Amazonian jungle of South America, each environment on Earth provides challenges: In some places it might be how to deal with high heat; in others, how to extract enough water from a parched landscape to stave off dehydration and death.

To make a more formidable impression on a Central American toad-eater snake (Xenodon rabdocephalus), a cane toad (Bufo marinus) inflates its lungs and angles its body toward its predator. If all else fails, the toad can spray its attacker with poison from glands on its body.

"The survival of the fittest which I have here sought to express in mechanical terms, is that which Mr. Darwin has called 'natural selection,' or the preservation of favored races in the struggle for life."

— HERBERT SPENCER 1820-1903

Principles of Biology

The final struggle of a Mozambique spitting cobra (Naja mossambica) is played out against the austere backdrop of Kenyan grassland, as the snake is attacked and quickly killed by a white-throated monitor lizard (Varanus albigularis).

Then there are the day-to-day issues that face animals no matter where they live—how to find food, move around, and avoid becoming a predator's next meal. For each of these daily activities, reptiles and amphibians have developed a myriad of techniques. There are lizards that walk on water, creatures that spray blood at attackers, and frogs that can freeze solid and survive weeks of suspended animation.

Of course, in nature nothing is permanent. As noted on pages 60 to 61, the dramatic decline in the numbers of amphibians in the last twenty years sounds a warning that even creatures as tough and resilient as these may not endure.

Defense Mechanisms

Life in the wild is tough. Most amphibians and reptiles are under constant threat from a variety of crafty predators. Snakes, however frightening they may be to some people, routinely are carried off by birds, while salamanders are attacked and eaten by larger amphibians, shrews, and even insects, to name just a few common enemies. Even the fearsome caiman is frequently squeezed to death by the South American green anaconda (*Eunectes murinus*). But all amphibians and reptiles, however small or seemingly vulnerable, have developed a few tricks to improve their chances of survival.

are often colored brown or gray to match the most common surface in their habitat.

Skin coloration can be remarkably complex and subtle. Many arboreal rain-forest lizards, among other reptiles, enjoy excellent camouflage from skin that mimics the

With skin that is virtually indistinguishable from moss and lichen, the Madagascar mossy leaf-tailed gecko (Uroplatus sikorae) can hide in plain sight.

KEEPING A LOW PROFILE

Perhaps the best way to avoid becoming a meal for a hungry predator is not to get noticed in the first place. The skin coloration of hundreds of amphibian and reptile species serves as camouflage, allowing individuals to fade into the background. Most arboreal snakes are brown or green, depending on whether they spend their time on open limbs or surrounded by foliage, while terrestrial snakes

moss, bark, and lichen found on the tree trunks in these regions. The casque-headed frog of Ecuador (*Hemiphractus proboscideus*) not only has skin that resembles the dead leaves in its habitat, but the frog's somewhat flat, sharp-edged head and limbs also have an uncanny resemblance to the shape of leaves as well.

ESCAPE ARTISTS

Numerous amphibians and reptiles rely on their mobility to elude predators. A leap from land into water is all it takes to carry a frog out of harm's way. Tree frogs can escape simply by jumping from one branch to another, interrupting the scent trail relied on by near-sighted predators such as snakes. In one of the most dramatic escape adaptations among reptiles, a genus of tree-dwelling Asian lizards (Draco) can glide to safety from high tree branches by pulling flaps of skin on the flanks tight to create crude wings.

Salamanders are usually slow movers, but they are capable of impressive bursts of speed when in danger. As they make their escape, many display unusual body movements. By coiling and uncoiling its body or flipping its tail while running away, the salamander not only puts distance between itself and a predator, but also confuses and intimidates the enemy.

SURVIVAL OF THE FOULEST

As a last resort when attacked, many amphibians and reptiles do whatever possible to seem

A Tail of Regeneration

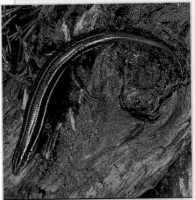

During an encounter with a predator, many lizards and some salamanders can voluntarily shed their tail. For up to several minutes, the tail continues to squirm about on the ground, distracting the predator and providing an opportunity for escape. In these species, the tail develops with one or more weak points that allow an easy break. Tail loss can save a life in the short run, but this comes at a price. During the months it takes for the tail to grow back, recovering individuals experience lower survival rates and reproductive output.

When grasped by a predator, the ribs of the sharp-ribbed newt (Pleurodeles waltl) stick through poisonous skin glands and inject toxins into the attacker.

The vibrant colors of the poison-arrow frog (above), a visual delight to human viewers, warn predators that this creature can secrete toxins from its skin. When threatened, the regal horned lizard (Phrynosoma solare) (right) can restrict blood flowing from its head until the pressure ruptures blood vessels around its eyes, spewing blood at its attacker.

unpalatable. Sometimes simply playing dead can be enough to cause a predator to lose interest and look for a fresher meal. Otherwise, more elaborate strategies are necessary. Certain lizards and snakes defecate profusely to put off predators. Most colubrid snakes not only excrete a particularly foul concoction from their anal glands but will then attempt to smear it on persistent attackers. When disturbed, almost all amphibians produce skin secretions that are either sticky, horrible-tasting, or poisonous. Some of the most deadly of these secretions are manufactured by the poison-arrow frogs of Central and South America. The tiny, colorful kokoi poison-arrow frog (*Phyllobates bicolor*) of Colombia, for example, produces a skin secretion so toxic

Intimidation Tactics

When immediate escape from a predator is impossible, many amphibians and reptiles resort to intimidation tactics to frighten or confuse the attacker. The Australian frilled lizard (*Chlamydosaurus kingii*), shown at left, inflates its body and displays a throat fan to give predators the impression that they're dealing with a much larger animal. Some snakes, notably various cobra species, inflate or expand their neck to create a more menacing hooded appearance. Some species rely on unusual markings to frighten predators. The false-eyed frog (*Physalaemus nattereri*) is one of several frog species with a pair of round markings on its back—normally hidden by its legs—that look like wide, staring eyes. When approached, it turns its back on the attacker, inflates its body, and elevates its hind end to reveal the eyespots.

Often the most venomous or poisonous species of amphibian and reptile species are brightly colored and easily detected. In such cases, the vivid colors are a warning to experienced predators not to bother again with these unsavory or dangerous creatures. Certain palatable or harmless species mimic the warning coloration of their noxious counterparts and trick predators into staying away from them as well. The harmless imitator salamander (*Desmognathus imitator*), found in the Great Smoky Mountains, mimics the red face markings of the region's poisonous Jordan's salamander (*Plethodon jordani*).

that 0.0000004 ounce (0.000011 g) can kill an adult human being.

The cane toad (*Bufo marinus*) of the southern hemisphere not only boasts a highly toxic skin secretion, but also can squirt the poison several feet into a predator's face from glands behind its head. However, most amphibians are not as efficient as the cane toad at deploying their protective toxins. Instead, when attacked, they simply present predators with the most noxious part of the body, often in an aggressive display. Salamanders with noxious glands on their head butt into predators or swing their head about wildly.

The sharp-ribbed newt (*Pleurodeles waltl*) has a high concentration of poisonous glands in its well-developed tail, which it lashes at its predators. When the newt is under attack, its sharp-pointed ribs stick out through the poison glands in the skin and inject pain-causing toxins into the predator's mouth.

Feeding

The egg-eating snake (Dasypeltis scabra) from Africa, like all snakes, has a specially hinged jaw that allows it to ingest its favorite food. With the egg firmly in its mouth, the snake punctures the shell with a bony projection at the back of its throat and swallows the contents. Afterward, the shell is regurgitated.

If the old saying "you are what you eat" extends to the animal kingdom, then many amphibians and reptiles must have multiple personalities. These creatures are often indiscriminate carnivores that devour almost any live food available, from insects and worms to birds and mammals. Some frog species even eat their own young, especially after a particularly bountiful breeding season.

There are clear advantages to this manner of eating. By gorging themselves in times of plenty, and because of their slow metabolism, amphibians and reptiles are able to survive long periods without food. And by adopting a highly varied diet, they are less likely to run out of food in the first place.

However, as is so often the case in nature, generalizations don't tell the whole story. Most snakes have a fairly specialized diet and some turtles are almost completely herbivorous, sticking largely to a plant-based diet. Other turtle species, along with a variety of lizards, eat a mixed diet of plant and animal food. As for carnivores, a few are very picky eaters. Such is the case with the African egg-eater (*Dasypeltis scabra*), a snake that, as its name suggests, eats only birds' eggs.

SENSES

Amphibians and reptiles rely on a variety of information in their hunt for food. As might be expected, predators with well-developed eyes depend heavily on visual cues, such as a glimpse of movement or a familiar shape, to locate prey. Frogs and true chameleons (family Chamaeleonidae) are highly visual predators. The chameleon's eyes can work independently, each scanning the environment for food. When prey is sighted—usually an insect or other invertebrate—the chameleon turns its head so that both eyes can focus on the prey. This produces the binocular vision necessary for the chameleon's expert use of its long, projectile tongue *(page 46)*.

In general, the sense of smell—the ability to analyze chemicals in the air—is used to detect the general location of food. Some reptiles have a specialized detector called a Jacobson's organ *(box, right)* to analyze this chemical information. Taste and touch are more important in identifying food items once they have been obtained or placed in the mouth. As well, some aquatic animals can locate prey by analyzing changes in water pressure with the lateral line system, a series of receptors located along the sides of the body. The importance of hearing among amphibian and reptile predators is not well understood, but the sense clearly plays a

Extrasensory Advantage

In addition to the five senses humans possess, a number of reptiles have an extra sense—sometimes two—to help them locate prey and identify predators and potential mates. With snakes and some lizards, the sensory arsenal includes a Jacobson's organ, located on the roof of the mouth. The snake gathers chemical molecules on its tongue by waving it in the air or touching it to the ground, then inserting the two tips of the tongue into the paired cavities of the Jacobson's organ. The sensory cells that line the organ process the signals and the information is analyzed by the brain. A few snake species, such as pit vipers and certain pythons, also have heat-sensitive facial pits. These thermoreceptors allow snakes hunting in total darkness to locate and strike accurately at prey by sensing its body heat.

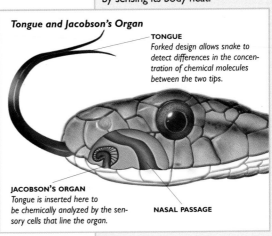

Tongue and Jacobson's Organ

TONGUE
Forked design allows snake to detect differences in the concentration of chemical molecules between the two tips.

JACOBSON'S ORGAN
Tongue is inserted here to be chemically analyzed by the sensory cells that line the organ.

NASAL PASSAGE

part. In particular, sensitivity to vibrations in the ground is a widespread adaptation.

Turtles, such as the eastern box (Terrapene carolina) shown at left, have varied diets, dining mostly on vegetation, but also nibbling at insects, worms, and even wild fruit.

FEEDING TECHNIQUES

Life as a herbivore has significant advantages: Vegetation never puts up a struggle. Animal prey is another matter, so carnivorous amphibians and reptiles have adopted a variety of techniques for catching and subduing their food. Many terrestrial animals, including most frogs, use their projectile tongues to retrieve prey. Once the prey has been identified and is within striking distance, the predator orients itself and flicks its tongue. The tip of the tongue snares the targeted creature with sticky saliva.

Holding itself in place with its prehensile tail, a common chameleon (Chamaeleo chamaeleo) flicks its tongue and snares an unsuspecting insect on a nearby leaf.

With a highly complex tongue musculature—to say nothing of a tongue that is often longer than the animal's body—the chameleon has the most impressive projectile-tongue technique in nature. Its tongue is supported by a rod, called the lingual process, and is shot from the mouth by an accelerator muscle at speeds that can exceed 16.5 feet (5 m) per second. The sticky tip of the tongue contracts to grasp the prey, then the tongue is retracted.

The entire maneuver is accomplished in the blink of an eye.

Slow-moving turtles feed primarily on vegetation and, depending on habitat and hunting skills, the odd high-protein item or two, such as fish, worms, or insect larvae. Most turtles forage lazily, but several species have developed techniques for

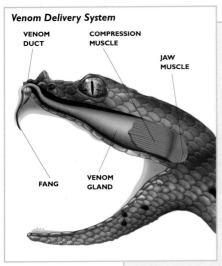

Venom Delivery System

VENOM DUCT

COMPRESSION MUSCLE

JAW MUSCLE

FANG

VENOM GLAND

Dangerous Snakes

With no arms or legs to grasp prey and rip it apart, and with teeth that are not designed for tearing and chewing, snakes have developed highly specialized techniques for making a meal of other animals. Many snakes, especially species that feed on invertebrates, frogs, or fish, simply seize their prey and swallow it whole. Other snakes use constriction to subdue prey. First, the snake strikes at the prey, grabbing it with its teeth. If the bite is secure, the snake begins looping its body around the animal, adjusting and tightening the coils. Scientists once believed that death was caused by suffocation, but actually the animal dies when the compression on the chest cavity causes the heart to stop. At this point, the snake loosens its grip and begins to swallow the prey head-first. Finally, some snakes subdue or kill their prey with venom: a complex mix of substances that acts on the blood, tissues, or nervous system. Most venomous snakes bite their prey with long, hollow teeth or fangs. The compression muscles in the jaw quickly contract and push the the venom through the venom ducts and the fangs into the puncture wound. Rattlesnakes keep their fangs tucked next to the roof of their mouth until needed, when the upper jaw bone rotates the fangs forward.

ambushing prey. The strange-looking matamata turtle (*Chelus fimbriatus*) lies in wait for fish to come near. Its lumpy, flattened shell, typically covered with algae, blends in perfectly with the surroundings, while highly sensitive skin flaps on its chin and neck detect the approach of small prey. When a fish swims within reach, the turtle juts out its neck, opens its oversized mouth and throat, and sucks the unsuspecting prey into its gullet along with a rush of water. In a more elaborate procedure, the alligator snapping turtle (*Macroclemys temmincki*) lures prey to its mouth with a wormlike appendage located at the tip of its tongue. The turtle remains motionless, hidden by its camouflage shell, and waits with its mouth open for a fish to go after the "worm." At precisely the right moment, the turtle clamps its jaws shut and, voilà, dinner is served.

The Problem With Water

Amphibians rarely drink water; instead, they absorb it through their permeable skin. Frogs, such as the Lehmann's poison-arrow frog (Dendrobates lehmanni) shown above, are aided by a thin patch of skin on their stomach that can absorb water even from moist earth.

Water, water everywhere; or nowhere at all. For reptiles and amphibians living in habitats ranging from ponds to deserts, the problem is sometimes finding enough water to survive. Often, though, an animal may actually have too much. Seldom drinking, frogs soak up water through permeable skin and must excrete it constantly to avoid becoming bloated. In a dry environment, a frog will lose water through its skin as fast as it would evaporate from an uncov-

ered bowl. Similarly, the permeable skin of salamanders allows water to pass through; a dry adult ensatina salamander (*Ensatina eschscholtzi*) can increase its weight 40 percent when placed in water.

Those amphibians that wander far from standing water face a different challenge: How to survive in dry areas with permeable skin? One solution, adopted by toads, is to thicken the skin to reduce evaporation. Some frogs add a relatively impermeable wax to their skin to reduce evaporation loss.

But not all their skin is protected. Toads have a baggy patch of skin, equipped with many blood vessels, on their substantial paunch, which they plump down on any moisture to soak it up. Some, such as the western spade-foot toad (*Scaphiophus hammondii*), can tolerate a remarkable degree of water loss before they "tank up" again, surviving a 60 percent decrease in body water.

Burrowing during the heat of the day is another means of reducing water loss. Both the African bull-

Water Collecting, Turtle-Style
The shell of some desert-dwelling turtles has been modified to collect rain. The outside parts of their shell are like gutters, channeling water forward to their front legs, which then direct the water into the animal's mouth.

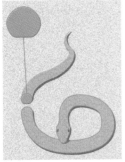 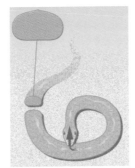 

Desert Viper Collecting Water
The Peringuey's adder (Bitis peringueyi) has a novel technique for obtaining water from its parched environment. The normally round shape of the snake (left) can be made flatter (center), which allows dew drops to collect more efficiently on its body. The snake then licks up the water and raises its head (right) to swallow.

frog (*Pyxicephalus adspersus*) and the Australian water-holding frog (*Cyclorana platycephala*) take this to an extreme by being active only during rainy periods. When it's dry in their desert environments, they dig deep into the ground, forming a cocoon around themselves by shedding outer layers of skin *(page 54)*. To survive long dormant periods, these cocooning species hold great amounts of water in their bladder. Australian aborigines dig for water-holding frogs, obtaining half a glass of pure water from each one.

REPTILES AND THEIR WATER QUEST

In contrast with the outer skin of most amphibians, the scaly skin of reptiles is a good barrier to water loss; some reptiles lose water three hundred to five hundred times more slowly than a water-dwelling frog. As a consequence, far more reptiles have colonized dry areas. Rather than soak up water through the skin, most terrestrial reptiles actively drink through their mouth.

To help conserve moisture, land-dwelling reptiles do not eliminate ammonia from their body by urinating as humans do. Instead, they convert the body waste into a semi-solid mass, which they then excrete.

In areas where standing water rarely forms, some species have adapted ingenious techniques for collecting water. Two lizard species, including Australia's thorny devil (*Moloch horridus*) and Asia's toad-headed agamid (*Phrynocephalus helioscopus*), have channels between their scales that transport dew from their body to their mouth. The shell of some desert-dwelling turtles has been modified to collect rain *(opposite)*, while at least one snake can alter its shape to collect life-saving dew *(above)*. In extremely dry desert conditions, reptiles may go for months without drinking. To survive, they extract water from food. Up to 70 percent of some plants, for example, is water.

49

Getting Around

Walking, running, hopping, swimming, slithering: Reptiles and amphibians move from place to place in almost every way imaginable. The only thing they don't do is fly—though some come close.

WALKING AND RUNNING

In four-legged walking, three limbs on the ground form a triangle of support while the fourth limb is moving. If the animal's center of gravity is outside this triangle, it will tend to fall off balance. For most slow to moderate walkers, such as salamanders and lizards, a lateral walking pattern *(right)*, with limbs on the same side moving in opposite directions, usually offers the largest base of support.

Turtles' vertebrae and ribs are fused to the bony part of their hard shell, making lateral flexion impossible. Instead, they capitalize on instability. A walking turtle will raise its back foot before its opposite front foot has touched down again. Unable to balance on two legs, the turtle falls forward and catches itself on the moving front foot.

This creates a rolling gait, but uses the force of gravity as an assist in forward propulsion.

Climbing shifts the effect of gravity to another dimension, and reptiles and amphibians have evolved a number of adaptations to meet various challenges. Tree frogs move in trees with the aid of specially adapted toes with enlarged pads or discs at the end. The cells on the surface of the pads are flat-topped and mucous is secreted between them. The thin, viscous layer is curved slightly inward and surface tension helps it adhere.

Striding Forward
In the lateral walking pattern of most salamanders and lizards, side-to-side twisting of the spine shifts the center of gravity (shown by a green dot in the illustrations) and increases the size of the support triangle, enhancing stability.

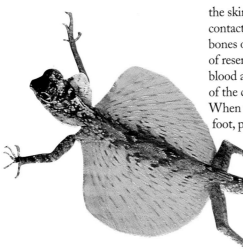

the skin that increase the area of contact with the surface. Under the bones of each toe is a sinus, a sort of reservoir that can be filled with blood and is separated from the rest of the circulatory system by a valve. When the gecko puts weight on the foot, pressure builds up inside the sinuses and in the network of blood vessels

Although not actually flying, the East Indian flying dragon (genus Draco) can execute a controlled glide of more than 150 feet (46 m), landing only a short distance below its launching point.

Chameleons, too, have feet specially adapted for climbing. Their toes are fused together in one group of two and another group of three on each foot. One of the sets faces forward, the other backward, enabling the animals to curl them together around tree branches as birds' feet do. In addition, chameleons have a prehensile tail, suitable for seizing or grasping, which they can use as a fifth support. Other species of lizards, including the giant Solomon Island prehensile-tail skink (*Corucia zebrata*) and some geckos, can also grip surfaces with their tail.

Geckos can even walk up sheer surfaces by means of overlapping plates, called lamellae, on the underside of their toes and a pressurizing system within their feet. The lamellae are covered with microscopic setae, spatula-shaped projections of

connecting them to the lamellae, forcing the lamellae and setae firmly against the surface. To release the pressure, each toe is raised from the tip toward the base.

To avoid predators, some amphibians and reptiles resort to running. The basilisk lizard (*Basiliscus basiliscus*) can even run on water. As its feet strike the water's surface, fringed scales on the sides of its toes increase the surface area of the feet. An air pocket forms behind the foot, reducing resistance from the water when the foot lifts. This allows the basilisk to move its legs very rapidly, creating an added momentum when it is running, which prevents it from breaking the surface tension of the water and sinking.

HOPPING AND LEAPING

The difference between hopping and leaping can be spectacular. A hop, characteristic of toads, involves taking off from the back feet and also landing on them, with the front legs landing almost simultaneously.

Relative to their size, frogs are able to leap incredible distances—the bullfrog (Rana catesbeiana) can jump nine times its body length, while the southern cricket frog (Acris gryllus) may travel up to thirty-six times its body length in one leap.

It usually covers only a short distance. A leap, a typical frog maneuver, also starts with takeoff from the back feet, but landing is on the front legs and chest, and usually a long way away. Frogs have legs particularly well adapted for leaping. All the bones of their back legs are long, their feet are elongated, and they have two extra "joints"—two bones of their ankles are extended and articulated separately from the front part of the foot. The bones of the pelvic girdle, where the legs join the spine, are also elongated, forming an extra joint at the top of the leg. These long, flexible back legs, combined with the specialized action of groups of leg muscles, provide maximum thrust. Not surprisingly, frogs that leap tend to have larger, more muscular back legs than frogs that usually walk, climb, or swim.

SWIMMING AND SLITHERING

In swimming, turtles use both pairs of legs in unison, moving the diagonally opposite front and back legs simultaneously to minimize movement from side to side. Webbing between the toes opens as the feet push backward, increasing drag and pushing the body forward.

By comparison, sea turtles, such as the leatherback turtle (*Dermochelys coriacea*), have developed front legs that look like paddles. As they swim, both front legs move together in a narrow figure-eight motion that makes the turtle look like it is flying underwater.

The form of snake locomotion we describe with the word "slither" is technically called lateral undulation. The snake moves in a curving fashion, but generates forward movement by pushing against various fixed points, such as surface irregularities, rocks, and stones, in its path. As the snake advances, body segments further along push against the same points. Some snakes, particularly on low-friction surfaces such as sand, move in a side-winding fashion: The body travels in a diagonal direction so that the snake looks as though it is rolling across the ground. A third form of motion, called rectilinear, employed by many large snakes such as boas and pythons, allows a snake to move in a virtually straight line: Scales grip the ground and pull the snake forward, while a muscular action travels in waves from the front of the body to the back.

PARACHUTING AND GLIDING

Some tree frogs, such as the Borneo flying frogs (*Rhacophorus* sp.) and the Wallace's flying frog (*Rhacophorus nigropalmatus*), get down to the ground quickly by parachuting out of the tree. They don't fly and they're not technically gliding since the angle of descent is steeper than forty-five degrees, but they're not simply falling either. Their limbs are extended out from their body, with their enlarged and webbed feet splayed to maximize resistance. Different species have different extents of control when parachuting and may be able to move to the left or right, turn to face in the opposite direction, or land some considerable distance from the base of the tree where they started.

The East Indian flying dragon (genus *Draco*) glides, moving through the air at angles as shallow as fifteen degrees. This controlled glide is made possible by two flaps of skin (patagia), one on each side of the body between the legs, that are supported by ribs and ligaments. The flaps open when the lizard jumps.

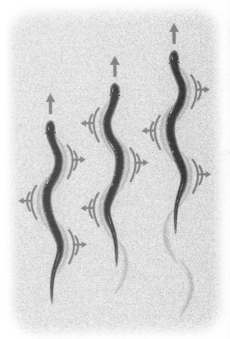

Pressing Ahead
For a snake to move forward in so-called lateral undulation, it must maintain a minimum of three contact points, which it presses against laterally. At least one of them must be on the side opposite the other two. Otherwise, the snake would move sideways instead of forward.

Dealing With Heat & Cold

Mammals and birds have high metabolic rates that allow them to maintain body temperatures above that of their surroundings. Although usually referred to as warm-blooded, these animals are more appropriately termed endotherms, meaning that their primary source of body heat is internal.

Reptiles and amphibians, on the other hand, produce very little such metabolic heat, relying instead on external sources of heat, such as the sun, to attain internal temperatures at which normal body functions will operate properly. This so-called ectothermic life offers one main advantage: A snake requires a tenth to a hundredth as much food as a mammal or bird of the same weight to stay alive. But this way of living also poses certain inescapable problems: principally, how to stay warm when it is cool—and cool when it is overly warm.

Every species of reptile and amphibian has an optimal temperature range within which it functions best. Below that, the animal is too cold and sluggish to move; above the critical maximum, the

Deep Sleep

Extreme weather gives rise to some extreme survival methods. In some hot, dry climates, several species of amphibians, including the lesser siren salamander (*Siren intermedia*) of North America and the Australian water-holding frog (*Cyclorana platycephala*) shown below, form a "cocoon" made of layers of shed skin. This waterproof cover completely encases the body, except for the nostrils and the mouth, and keeps the animal from dehydrating after it has burrowed underground to estivate. Once the rains return, the animal breaks free from the cocoon and emerges, ready to feed and breed.

In the cold winters of Canada and northern United States, five species of frogs, including the wood frog (*Rana sylvatica*), actually freeze solid. Increased levels of glucose or glycerol produced by the liver protect the cells from exploding as 60 percent of the extracellular body fluids freezes. Blood circulation ceases, the heart stops pumping, and body fermentation processes are the only thing that keeps the frogs alive. Once spring and warmer temperatures come, they thaw out and metabolize excess levels of glucose or glycerol before resuming their normal activities.

animal loses muscular coordination and can no longer evade conditions that cause overheating and death.

Optimal temperature ranges vary significantly. Species from temperate climates, and amphibians as a group, are typically able to function at much lower temperatures than those from deserts or tropical climates. Species from constant equatorial climates or warm waters have much narrower optimal temperature ranges, while high-altitude species are adapted to cooler optimal temperatures than the range of similar species from lower altitudes.

Like other reptiles and amphibians, turtles face a constant struggle to keep their body at an optimal temperature. Sunbathing will bring their temperature up; once they become too warm, a quick dip in the water may be needed to cool off.

THERMOREGULATION

Sitting on the protruding tip of a rock in the shallow waters of a lake, a turtle is quietly sunning itself, with legs and neck fully outstretched from its shell. Gradually its body temperature climbs to the temperature at which its metabolism is the most efficient for such needs as foraging, feeding, and digesting. At this point, the turtle will enter the cool water again, both to avoid overheating and to resume its activities. When its body temperature drops too low, it repeats the process.

Thermoregulation, or the action of controlling its own body temperature by external means, is a daily concern in the life of reptiles and amphibians. Thermal exchanges constantly occur between the animal and the air that surrounds it, the surface it sits on, nearby objects, and the sun. Two different means of thermoregulation are commonly used to achieve proper body temperatures: behavioral and physiological.

The primary concern for diurnal reptiles and amphibians on emerging from their night retreats is to increase their body temperature.

Heat can be gained by radiation, conduction, or convection *(left)*. How much of the available energy is taken up by the animal depends on such factors as skin absorption or reflection, the amount of body surface exposed to the source of heat, and the angle at which radiation strikes the body. Conversely, heat loss can occur by radiation, conduction, convection, evaporation, and the contact surface between the animal and the ground. Amphibians from cooler climates or habitats are acclimatized to lower temperatures and so can attain an optimal body temperature more quickly and easily.

Some snakes and lizards alter their body shape and position to warm up or cool down. Others extend only their head from a burrow or dugout to gradually warm their brain, thereby increasing their reaction time before they emerge to continue basking. Aquatic turtles and crocodilians move from deep, cool water to bask or float in warmer, shallower waters. Many species of lizards and snakes absorb heat during the day through contact with the underside of rocks and logs.

These behavioral adaptations are complemented by many physiological changes. During early-day basking, many species can shunt blood

Here Comes the Sun

By facing the sun and thus minimizing the amount of solar radiation it receives (top), a reptile can reduce the warming effects of direct sunlight. Turning sideways increases the surface area exposed to the sun's warming rays; some reptiles can even spread their ribs to make the body more circular. Another posture technique involves angling the body toward the sun. In addition to direct radiation from the sun, heat can be gained by conduction from the ground or a nearby rock, or by convection from the ambient air (bottom).

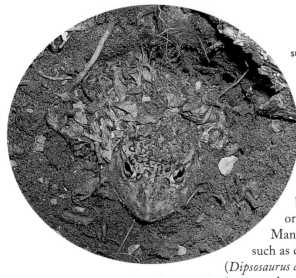

A giant bullfrog (Pyxicephalus adspersus) emerges from underground, where it had burrowed to avoid the midday heat.

flow to the smaller vessels under the skin by muscular action to carry heat more efficiently throughout the body—even parts that are still under cover. Other animals can alternately lighten or darken their color to absorb or reflect heat.

In addition to activity, the size and mass of a creature influences thermoregulation. Large-mass reptiles lose heat less rapidly from their core and can thus maintain higher energy levels. Leatherback turtles can maintain internal body temperatures significantly above ambient environmental temperatures, allowing the creatures to range far north of what otherwise might seem to be their normal reptilian limits.

AVOIDING EXTREMES

To avoid extremely warm temperatures, most reptiles and amphibians are nocturnal during certain periods of the year, while others emerge to bask only early or late in the day. Many desert species, such as desert iguanas (*Dipsosaurus dorsalis*), burrow in the ground to shelter themselves from intense midday heat. To cool down, the sand-diving lizard (*Meroles anchietae*) of the African Namib Desert elevates two legs at a time when the ground gets too hot. If this action fails to do the trick, the lizard quickly runs and plunges into the sand to escape the heat. Basking frogs bathe more frequently and discharge more mucous from their skin cells to increase evaporative cooling. In the most arid and warmest climates, summer dormancy, or estivation, is also employed by some species to avoid dealing with very hot temperatures. Some reptiles and amphibians respond to extreme conditions—both hot and cold—by dormancy, hibernation or estivation. A few species even resort to a form of suspended animation *(page 54)* in order to survive.

Sounding Off

Like all calling frogs and toads, the American toad inflates its vocal sac to amplify and "color" the sound of its call.

With a few exceptions, such as frogs and toads, most amphibians and reptiles aren't highly vocal creatures. The main ways these animals communicate with each other is with chemical, visual, and tactile signals. Still, sounds play a significant role in the life of a surprising number of species. Researchers have observed that even the neotropical caecilian (*Dermophis*), a wormlike creature that spends most of the time burrowing underground, emits soft yelps or squeaks and barely audible smacking and clicking sounds. It seems that these animals orient themselves with the sounds (just as bats do) and use them to identify each other for mating. As for amphibians and reptiles well-known for sound communication—frogs and alligators among them—the variety of sounds used can be remarkably elaborate.

FROG TALK

With their familiar nighttime croaking, male frogs and toads are the most conspicuous amphibian vocalizers. The basic function of their so-called advertisement call is to bring the sexes together for mating. But there's more to the sound than meets the ear—at least the human ear. Many frogs actually make a variety of croaking sounds. Male frogs may use one call to attract a mate and another more aggressive call to keep other males away. Sometimes both sounds are made during the same calling sequence. The Puerto Rican coqui (*Eleutherodactylus coqui*), for example, is named for its two-part call, which begins with an aggressive, territorial "co" note and ends with a series of "qui" notes that attract females: "co-qui-qui-qui-qui." Researchers have noted that if a male comes within about twenty inches (50 cm) of a calling frog, the latter drops the "qui" sound and calls out a series of threatening "co" notes.

Some male frogs have a different short-range courting call, to which females respond with their own reciprocal call. This allows couples to find each other in a crowded breeding area. Certain frog species are also known to produce fright calls when confronted by a predator and distress calls when attacked.

GATOR GAB

Alligators, the most vocal of the reptiles, use a number of sounds at every stage of their life, including a complex set of signals during mating. To defend territory and attract mates, male and female American alligators (*Alligator mississippiensis*) produce a loud, repetitive roar that can be heard more than six hundred feet (180 m) away. Just before the male makes this sound, he emits a low-frequency signal that creates underwater waves. A chorus of males frequently bellows for more than an hour at a time during breeding season.

In an aggressive display that often leads up to a physical fight over a mate, the male alligator sometimes aggressively smacks the water with his head. Following a physical confrontation, the winner holds his body high in the water, while the loser adopts a passive posture or swims away. When a female approaches the victorious male, both begin emitting unusual raspy vocalizations and courting rituals begin. If a female eventually loses interest, she makes a distinct growling noise and retreats under

> ### Lizard Language
> Geckos are unique among lizards in having well-developed vocal cords and the ability to produce sounds more complex than basic gasps and hisses. Indeed, some gecko species have an elaborate repertoire of chirps and clicks adapted to a variety of social interactions from territorial competition among males to mating.

water or swims off. While the American alligator is the most studied of the world's crocodilians, similar behavior has been reported in other species.

Not-yet-hatched baby alligators use vocal signals to communicate among themselves and with newly hatched siblings in the nest. The calls may help to synchronize egg hatching and they also attract the mother back to the nest. Later, during the year or two that young alligators remain with their mother, they may produce distress calls that elicit protective responses from both parents.

The American alligator emits a range of vocal sounds, from the raspy vocalizations and bellowing of adults to the distress calls of the young. Even baby alligators still in the egg communicate with others in the nest.

59

A Fragile Existence

In the early 1990s, scientists began to notice strange deformities in frogs—extra toes, even extra legs. They also knew that the number of amphibians in general had been plummeting since the 1970s. Amphibians that had once been plentiful had become much rarer. And some species had disappeared altogether. That trend, which con-

Deformities in frogs have become more pronounced in recent years, leading many scientists to wonder what changes in the natural world are prompting these abnormalities.

tinues unabated, has alarmed some scientists because of amphibians' extreme sensitivity to changes in the environment. Is the decline an indication of a planet that is becoming increasingly toxic to life in general, human life included? Is something seriously amiss in our natural world?

It's not difficult to come up with a list of possible culprits for amphibian decline. Habitat loss appears to be one of the most obvious. Swamps are being drained for new developments, forests are being logged, and grassland is going under the plow. And yet amphibians are also disappearing from pristine areas where there is no visible disturbance. This has led many biologists to suspect that airborne environmental contamination may be behind the

widespread declines. Exposure to contaminants may make amphibians more vulnerable to forces that they are normally able to battle. There is also a risk that chemicals such as acid rain and pesticides are causing hormonal imbalances, increasing sterility or producing deformed or sterile offspring. Increased UV radiation resulting from depletion of the ozone layer has also been implicated in reducing the survival and development of amphibian eggs and larvae.

Other problems result from introduced animals, such as bullfrogs and fish. These species are usually brought in from other areas for commercial or recreational purposes and sometimes end up outcompeting native animals, feeding on them, or transmitting diseases.

With so many factors at work it becomes extremely difficult to pinpoint a primary cause—assuming that there is one. Contradictions abound. For example, some amphibian populations may decline in ponds after predatory fish are introduced and yet the same species may coexist well with the same fish in other nearby ponds.

Another fact to be kept in mind is that declines and extinctions are not new: They occur naturally in animal populations. Perhaps, as some biologists suggest, the reductions in populations over the last twenty years are natural and are simply more noticeable because of our increased awareness.

REPTILES AT RISK, TOO

Reptiles face similar threats, particularly habitat loss, although their numbers have not declined as radically as amphibians. Reptiles seem to suffer most from conscious human actions, such as the killing of turtles and tortoises for food and the harvesting of poisonous snakes for their venom. Then there is the black market animal trade. Apart from providing ingredients for exotic dishes, traditional medicines, and aphrodisiacs, dealers can make up to $30,000 on the black market for rare or endangered reptiles.

Efforts are being made to overcome some of these threats. Countries such as Costa Rica restrict harvesting and protect the breeding ground beaches of sea turtles. Captive breeding programs in the Galapagos Islands of Ecuador artificially incubate eggs of tortoises and raise them to a minimum size that is less vulnerable to predators before releasing them into the wild. Salamander reserves have been set up in the United States. And many nations are now party to the Convention on International Trade in Endangered Species (CITES) of wild fauna and flora, which restricts the movement of endangered species or products made from them throughout the world.

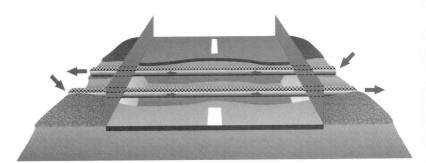

Tunnel System
Untold numbers of reptiles and amphibians are killed every year crossing highways.
To reduce this toll, engineers in Europe have designed an animal "crosswalk" that funnels
reptiles and amphibians into a pipe and allows them to pass safely under a road.

Reptile & Amphibian Pharmacopoeia

With their tinctures of toad and vials of snake oil, the traveling medicine men of the last century may have been more savvy than many people thought. Scientists today are recognizing that substances produced by reptiles and amphibians provide an extraordinary pharmacopoeia, with the potential to treat a wide range of human ills.

For centuries, healers around the world have treated patients with frog secretions, lizard fat, snake venom, and toad skins. They've made medicinal broths from snakes, infection salves from lizards, some remarkable mind enhancers from frogs and toads, and even a contraceptive out of crocodile dung. Observations in the past have suggested that some of these remedies were actually effective. Today scientists are busy isolating many of the powerful chemicals reptiles and amphibians secrete.

Ironically, it's the very vulnerability of some of these species that makes for such rich chemistry. Take amphibians, for example. With their relatively thin skin, they have had to rely on a host of

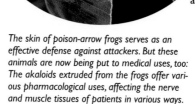

The skin of poison-arrow frogs serves as an effective defense against attackers. But these animals are now being put to medical uses, too: The akaloids extruded from the frogs offer various pharmacological uses, affecting the nerve and muscle tissues of patients in various ways.

toxic, or bad-smelling and -tasting skin secretions to ward off prey.

Toxins from the brightly colored poison-arrow frogs of Ecuador, used for centuries on the tips of Indians' arrows or blow-pipe darts, contain the makings of a powerful analgesic: Tests have shown that it's one hundred times more powerful than morphine—and non-sedative and probably non-addictive as well.

Some scientists believe that a particularly sticky mucous from other frogs may provide a way to bind together damaged organs that can't be stitched, while the powerful substances that ensure frogs' moist skin remains bacteria-free are now being studied as antibacterial and even antiviral agents. The bicolored tree frog (*Phyllomedusa bicolor*) of Brazil secretes a substance that affects cell communication, potentially revolutionizing research on Alzheimer's disease and depression. Scientists were prompted to study it after anthropologists came back with stories of how certain Brazilian Indians would rub self-inflicted burns with the frog's secretions and then go into a

As well as serving as the source of anti-venom serum for treating snake bites, snake venom is being studied for its pharmacological and diagnostic uses, including its effects on blood coagulation, blood pressure regulation, and nerve and muscle impulse transmission.

coma. When they woke up, they could hunt all day without getting hungry or tired and their arrows never seemed to miss a mark.

With powerful secretions of their own, many toads have been called movable drug stores. In the past, violinists would touch toads to cover their fingers with a substance to keep their skin dry. The Chinese have used adrenaline in dried toad skins for centuries to increase patients'

low blood pressure. Substances that paralyze the respiratory system and overstimulate the heart rate of any animal unwise enough to take a toad into its mouth are now being used in studies on the heart and nervous system, while a substance in the neotropical cane toad (*Bufo marinus*) is being analyzed as a possible weapon in the fight against heart disease, mental illness, and certain cancers.

Experimenters have even found that the properties of certain toads make for a unique recreational drug. The hallucinogenic highs obtained from licking the parotoid glands of these toads or smoking their dried toxin have been described as anything from a slight buzz to "a rocket trip into the void."

The Choco Indians of South America use the poison from toxic frogs to coat the tips of their blow darts. One frog can provide enough poison to coat fifty darts.

BACKYARD
& BEYOND

IN THE HOME

Reptiles and amphibians can make fascinating pets, but may present some unfamiliar challenges. This section explains what every new owner needs to know, from choosing the right pet to placing it in a setting that best mimics its natural environment.

The interest in keeping reptiles and amphibians as pets has increased considerably in recent years. And with good reason. The variety of species available, the array of shapes and colors exhibited, the unusual behavioral traits, and the ubiquitous curiosity value have all contributed to the mounting popularity. For a new pet owner, the choice is daunting: Where to begin?

The first step is to research as much as you can. Books, herpetological magazines and societies, and the Internet are good places to start. In particular, pay attention to a species' preferences—climatic (temperature, humidity, and lighting), environmental (habitat and living space), and social (is it solitary or gregarious?). Certain reptile and amphibian species are more difficult to look after than others, making them suitable only for experienced keepers. Chameleons, for example, have exacting requirements when it comes to space, temperature, and vitamin and mineral needs. Emerald tree boas (*Corallus caninus*) and Central American toads from the genus *Atelopus* are also demanding pets. As a beginner, start off with a popular and easily kept species; this will give you invaluable experience in learning about what is involved in looking after a reptile or amphibian pet. The corn snake (*Elaphe guttata guttata*), the leopard gecko (*Eublepharis macularius*), the inland bearded dragon (*Pogona vitticeps*), and the arboreal White's tree frog (*Litoria caerulea*) are just a few of the many good choices. But be aware that even some popular species may need considerable attention, perhaps because they demand more food, need more cleaning, or have more specific climate requirements.

Some species, such as the White's tree frog (Litoria caerulea), make better first-time pets than others, as their needs are few and easily met.

BUYING YOUR PET

The next step is figuring out where to buy your pet. A good starting point is the local pet store, more and more of which seem to be offering reptiles and amphibians. The species they sell are usually popular and not too demanding. Also, because of the small numbers the stores usually keep, specimens are normally well cared for. On the downside, such outlets are often unable to supply detailed information on the species they offer, making it especially important for you to read up on your prospective purchase before you buy.

If you are interested in an uncommon species, you will probably have to consider other suppliers, such as a specialist reptile and amphibian retailer or a private breeder. The variety of species available through these sources is often impressive. Breeders can also help you with tips on looking after the animals they sell. The best way to locate such a source is by studying the advertisements in reptile and amphibian magazines, such as *Vivarium*, searching the World Wide Web, or joining a local, national, or international reptile and amphibian society. Most societies publish a newsletter where fellow hobbyists advertise their surplus specimens and captive-bred offspring. Society meetings are also a place where hobbyists meet and sometimes sell their surplus stock.

Providing your pet with the right home and the proper heating and lighting equipment will go a long way toward keeping it healthy.

Specialist suppliers may be located many miles from where you live, making it difficult to view your pet before you purchase. They may offer a mail-order service. Avoid buying your pet this way unless you have actually seen the premises, the conditions in which the specimens are kept, and the overall quality of the specimens. Or, look for a good recommendation from a knowledgeable source.

Historically, another method of acquiring reptiles and amphibians has been to capture your own from the wild. Today, however, with habitat loss, increasing pressure from over-collection for the pet trade, human encroachment, and stringent new laws severely restricting or prohibiting collecting native reptiles and amphibians, this practice is no longer considered acceptable. Perhaps the only exception is collecting a few tadpoles of a common frog or toad from a local pond. Raising a tadpole through its developmental stages to a healthy adult is a rewarding achievement with great educational value for children.

CAPTIVE-BRED VERSUS WILD-CAUGHT

Specimens from most of the popular species as well as from an increasing number of rare species are now being produced through captive-breeding programs, making it no longer necessary to purchase wild-caught specimens. In addition to the obvious ethical considerations of not contributing to the

further depletion of reptiles and amphibians in the wild, there are practical reasons for choosing captive-bred pets. Wild-caught species are more likely to be host to various parasites and bacterial and viral agents, which, although normally harmless in their natural environment, will become magnified when the specimen is transferred to the stressful environment of a vivarium. Captive-bred specimens are accustomed to the artificial environment of captivity from day one. In addition, if you buy your specimen from a breeder, you may be able to receive a life history for a specimen, such as its age, sex, feeding, and skin-shedding frequency. A hazard of purchasing a live-caught specimen is that the creature may be nearing the end of its life span.

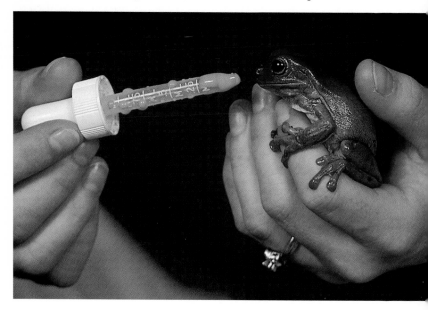

OTHER CONSIDERATIONS

Even with a popular captive-bred species, there may be local laws that govern whether you can legally keep that particular species in captivity. A prime example is the American bullfrog (*Rana catesbeiana*), which is banned in some places because of its invasive nature. Introduced indiscriminately in new territories, the bullfrog has destroyed fauna and driven other amphibians out of their natural habitat. Check local and state laws before acquiring your reptile or amphibian. A local library or county or state council is usually a good place to start.

Before you make your purchase, take some time to study the specimen's external appearance; this will give good indications as to its health. The skin should be unblemished, bright, and unbroken. No limbs or appendages should be missing. Pay particular attention to the mouth. It should be free from tears and swellings. Also, the cloaca, or vent region, should not display unusual secretions or sores. The eyes represent an excellent indication of the health of your prospective pet: They should be full and sparkling and not sunken.

AN UNWANTED PET

Perhaps your snake has become too much trouble to care for, has outgrown its vivarium, or you are no longer interested in having it. What should you do? First of all, ask people you know whether they would be interested in keeping it. If not, contact local animal rehabilitation centers, many of which try to provide homes for unwanted exotic creatures. You could also advertise your pet in a reptile and amphibian society newsletter or specialist magazine. Or, a pet or specialist supplier might take it off your hands.

Whatever you do, do not release your pet in the wild. It is almost certainly illegal to do this, regardless of whether the animal is a native species or not. The specimen might introduce a contagion that could decimate a local population or spread to other species. There is also the very real threat that, like the American bullfrog or the cane toad (*Bufo marinus*), it may wreak havoc in its new home, decimating the populations of native reptile or amphibian species.

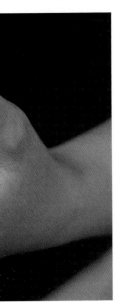

Like cats, dogs, and other more conventional pets, amphibians and reptiles sometimes need the attention of a veterinarian. Here, a White's tree frog (Litoria caerulea) is administered the antibiotic Amoxicillin.

69

A Place of Their Own

The best place to keep an amphibian or reptile pet is in a vivarium—a vented, aquarium-like container. Vivariums are available in a variety of materials, shapes, and sizes.

To choose the right one for your pet, consider the natural habitat and way of life of the species you plan to keep. A simple plastic or Plexiglas™ vivarium is ideal for rearing small snakes, salamanders,

A few carefully placed rocks re-create the kind of hiding place many desert reptile species look for in the wild. A covering of sand on the floor completes the scene. A full-spectrum fluorescent light bulb, housed in the fixture along the back of the lid, provides the same kind of light produced by the sun.

and newly metamorphosed frogs. More elaborate models, with built-in light fixtures and space for a heating pad under the floor, are also very popular. For aquatic animals, you'll need a standard glass aquarium. These are available with a wide range of specialized heating, lighting, and water-filtration accessories.

A glass aquarium tank is also a good choice for many terrestrial species. However, you may need to change the lid. Replacements are available that prevent escape and provide good ventilation and easy access to the tank. Whether you purchase a vivarium lid separately or not, look for one with a small opening where you can introduce food without having to open the full lid, and make sure it has a latch or lock to hold the top firmly in place.

If you need a larger vivarium for a terrestrial species, a vivarium made mostly of wood or melamine is a lighter and less expensive alternative to glass. These models usually have sliding or hinged glass doors on one side, or a glass front and a hinged lid. To prevent mold and rot, wipe down the interior of a wood vivarium regularly with a damp cloth and make sure all joints are sealed with a silicone-based sealant.

Plants and wood chips on the floor help create a humid environment. A hollowed-out tree stump serves as a place to hide. Built-in fluorescent lights can be hooked up to a timer to provide the right balance between light and darkness over a twenty-four hour period.

Regardless of the material you choose, your vivarium should be sturdy and provide enough space for your reptile or amphibian to move about freely. For a medium-sized snake, allow at least a square foot of floor space per foot of body length—double that amount for most lizards. Climbing species need more vertical space. If your pet is a juvenile, choose a model big enough for a full-grown adult—or be prepared to buy a larger vivarium later on. The vivarium should be escape-proof, both for your amphibian or reptile, as well as for any live food it eats. It's a good idea to have a second vivarium on hand—it can be smaller and quite basic—so you have somewhere to put your pet when cleaning or repairing the main container.

Many amphibians and some reptiles need a humid environment. This calls for a vivarium made from a waterproof material such as glass, plastic, or Plexiglas™. Avoid reducing or closing off ventilation to increase humidity. This can trigger respiratory problems and promote bacterial and fungal growth as well as the buildup of various gaseous products of metabolism. Humidity monitors and mist-spraying devices are available to maintain proper moisture levels.

FURNISHING YOUR VIVARIUM
Many reptiles need nothing more than a wooden hiding box, a few decorative rocks, a ceramic water dish, and newspaper, sand, or gravel on the floor. However, some reptiles demand a more accurate reproduction of their natural habitat. Many frogs and toads, such as poison-dart frogs and mantellas, require a heavily planted vivarium with mossy ground cover and a source of running water. Specialized pet stores sell miniature waterfalls for this purpose. Newts and sala-manders, too, also need a mossy environment and plenty of cover in the form of creeping plants, rocks, and branches. For semi-aquatic species such as turtles, add a dry spot above the water line, such as a rock or a float, where they can climb up and bask out of the water.

Heating & Lighting

As ectotherms—creatures that are dependent on external heat sources for raising their body temperature—amphibians and reptiles are particularly sensitive to heat and light. Do some research into your pet's natural environment, and equip the vivarium with heating and lighting equipment to re-create these conditions as closely as possible.

often do. Angle the light toward one side of the vivarium. This way the reptile can more easily find a comfortable temperature band. Bare bulbs must be shrouded in mesh to prevent burns since the surface of a spotlight bulb can reach dangerously high temperatures. Another concentrated heat source is a ceramic infrared emitter bulb.

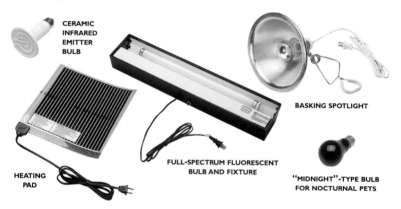

CERAMIC INFRARED EMITTER BULB

BASKING SPOTLIGHT

FULL-SPECTRUM FLUORESCENT BULB AND FIXTURE

HEATING PAD

"MIDNIGHT"-TYPE BULB FOR NOCTURNAL PETS

HEATING NEEDS

Each species functions best within a certain temperature range. However, this doesn't mean that all species require supplementary heating. In fact, most newts and salamanders, as well as many temperate frogs and toads, dislike high temperatures. In some cases, you may have to locate a vivarium in a cool room or install refrigeration equipment to simulate hibernation conditions.

Reptiles that normally spend a significant amount of time basking need a concentrated heat source. An incandescent spotlight will

It screws into a light-bulb socket, but produces only heat.

When an incandescent spotlight or emitter bulb is insufficient, you'll need an additional heat source. Radiant heating pads are the most popular choice. The surface of these units never gets too hot, making them a safe source of heat. However, they should be connected to a thermostat for precise control. Some models cool down at night to mimic temperature changes experienced in the wild. Place the heating pad beneath the vivarium floor for lizards and snakes that normally derive heat from the surface they rest on. In a

Handling Your Pet

Handle reptiles and amphibians only when necessary, such as during health inspections or when cleaning the vivarium. Wash your hands with anti-bacterial soap before and again after. Reptiles, in particular, can carry salmonella bacteria or other infectious agents. Humans can also infect reptiles with bacterial or viral agents. Amphibians have delicate, moist skin, so handle them with wet hands. Hold small lizards and snakes on the edge of your hand and gently pinch a lizard's hindleg or the snake's body between your thumb and forefinger. To handle larger snakes and lizards, gently pick them up at mid-body and provide ample support from below with one or both hands. An alternative is to coax your amphibian or reptile into a plastic container.

heavily planted tropical vivarium, you can fasten the pad to the side. Remember that higher temperatures make for a drier environment. So, if you're keeping tropical rainforest species, you may need a more frequent misting schedule.

LIGHTING REQUIREMENTS

Nocturnal reptiles and amphibians, such as geckos and salamanders, are used to little or no direct lighting. A reddish or blue "midnight"-type bulb allows you to see these animals without disturbing them. For most frogs and toads that inhabit the dense undergrowth of woodlands and forests, install a low-wattage, incandescent bulb. Species that spend long periods of time in the sun require full-spectrum fluorescent tubes. This kind of lighting, which includes ultraviolet wavelengths, acts as a substitute for sunlight and allows these species to mobilize and synthesize calcium, phosphorus, and vitamin D_3. Without it, tortoises and certain lizards, such as chameleons, can develop metabolic bone disease. Position the vivarium so it gets as much natural light as possible without risking overheating. Fluorescent lights of any kind are also brighter and cooler than incandescent bulbs of the same wattage.

The number of hours of light a species needs in a twenty-four hour period, or "photoperiod," must also be considered. Species from non-equatorial regions experience seasonal shifts in photoperiod. Mimicking this natural photoperiod in captivity may be necessary to stimulate reproductive behavior, although most species adapt well to a cycle of twelve hours of light and twelve of darkness.

Food & Feeding

To maintain any type of reptile or amphibian in good health, you must provide a balanced diet that offers all the necessary nutrients, including calcium, essential vitamins, minerals, and trace elements. Fortunately, many species are adaptable and will take a host of different food types. Certain reptiles, such as skinks, iguanas, and various turtles and tortoises, are omnivorous or herbivorous. Determine the vegetation your specimen prefers by offering it a number of different types. Even individuals of a single species may favor dissimilar foods. Certain species are far more selective. A few carnivores will eat only one type of prey. For the majority of species, the keeper's life has been made easier by the advent of specialist reptile and amphibian live-food laboratories, various freeze-dried foods, and a range of supplementary vitamin/mineral preparations.

Laboratory-bred live foods include various cricket species, locusts, beetles and their larvae (such as mealworms, buffalo worms, superworms), moth larvae, various earthworms, paramecium (a type of protozoa), bloodworms, brine shrimp, and a host of fruitfly strains. Certain snakes and salamanders are partial to types of fish that can easily be obtained from tropical fish outlets, where they are sold as "feeder fish" for eel and piranha keepers.

Larger foods offered by some laboratories range from baby to adult mice, rats, gerbils, rabbits, and day-old chicks. This food must always be offered pre-killed. Many countries have a law that prevents the feeding of live warm-blooded vertebrates to reptiles and amphibians.

Special diets for special needs: An anemic green iguana is spoonfed tofu, a source of iron.

PROPER NUTRIENTS

Although the range of foods available to the hobbyist has grown remarkably over the last few years, a complete diet usually requires more.

Most laboratory-bred items must be treated with supplementary nutrients. The simplest method is to coat the prey with a multivitamin/mineral and calcium preparation. Numerous preparations are available—in both liquid and powdered forms. Check the calcium-to-phosphorus ratio; it should be two to one. To coat the prey, place a small quantity of powdered nutrients in a container, add the prey, then gently shake the container until the prey is coated. Or, you can place the prey in the container first, then lightly spray it with a suitable liquid preparation.

Green grapes and mealworms may be an unappetizing combination to the human eye, but your lizard will lap it up.

Larger foods, such as pre-killed rodents, offer nearly complete nutrition. However, from time to time, perhaps one meal a week, it can be a good idea to lightly dust these items with supplementary nutrients or inject a solution of nutrients into the prey body.

The disadvantage of these methods is that certain species dislike the taste of the powder or liquid nutrients and will reject the food. When this happens, the prey must be "gut-loaded." This involves actually feeding live prey with food treated with a multivitamin/mineral preparation.

Freeze-dried preparations in pellet or cake forms are also readily available. However, while they contain added nutrients, experts advise that they be used as just one part of a varied diet.

For insectivorous reptiles and amphibians, consider collecting your own food. You can provide a nutritious diet with a combination of springtails and other leaf-litter invertebrates, aphids, termites, beetles, spiders, gnats, mosquitoes, caterpillars, moths, crickets, and earthworms. Just make sure that the backyard, field, or woodland where you gather the food is free from pesticide or herbicide treatment. If you have access to only one or two of these foods, you will also need to add supplements.

If your pet experiences health problems, your vet may recommend a special short-term diet.

Whatever you feed your reptile or amphibian, avoid overfeeding. Certain amphibians and reptiles are gluttons that will keep eating until they become obese. Also make sure that food items are not too big. This will prevent your pet from choking on its food or even becoming the prey.

IN THE WILD

While it's true that a vivarium or a zoo can allow you to observe an animal close up, nothing can match the thrill of spotting—and identifying—a reptile or amphibian in the outdoors. All you need is some very basic equipment and an idea of where to look.

One of the best ways to learn about reptiles and amphibians is to observe them in their natural habitat. You can do this by yourself or as part of a herpetological society or a naturalist club. On any field trip, remember to comply with the regulations of parks and reserves, and to ask permission before entering private property.

FIRST THINGS FIRST

The first step to a successful outing is to do advance research on the species found in the area you are planning to visit. Good bookstores and libraries offer a selection of field guides. Read up on the species to find out how they live so you'll know the spots where you are most likely to find specimens, such as in trees, around water, on the forest floor, or under rocks or logs. To find the most promising sites, take some time to become familiar with the area. Keep in mind, though, that amphibians and reptiles can be found almost

anywhere in many habitats—if you look hard enough. It's also wise to make sure you can identify any venomous species found in the area you are visiting; you'll want to give any poisonous species a safe berth. In addition to an authoritative field guide, you'll need a good pair of binoculars (choose a model with a short minimum-focusing distance), camera gear, a pencil, and a notebook to keep a record of what you have seen.

OUT AND ABOUT

Now that you're equipped and ready to head out into the field, where do you begin? Aim for specific groups of reptiles and amphibians, or precise habitats, and start looking.

Turtles and crocodilians are usually found in or around water. Use your binoculars to scan the shores and protruding rocks or logs in lakes, ponds, rivers, and canals for basking individuals. They will often dive in the water at the slightest disturbance, so approach them slowly. Day-active

"In the parched path/I have seen the good lizard/ (one drop of crocodile)/ meditating."
— FREDERICO LORCA (1898-1936)
The Old Lizard

If you join a herpetological society, you can participate in field trips and benefit from the knowledge of more experienced reptile and amphibian observers.

Be very careful when searching in an area where venomous species are present. Use a sturdy metal hook or a potato rake instead of your hands to overturn objects on the ground. This reduces the possibility of being bitten. Remember that any object you move should be put back in its original position so that the animals can continue to benefit from the microclimate created underneath.

snakes and lizards that forage in the open can also be fast and excitable. Again, binoculars will help you spot them before they see you.

Some groups, such as skinks, geckos, king snakes, and many species of tropical snakes, are mostly nocturnal or hide underground in hot weather. Look for them by lifting rocks, logs, and debris and inspecting vegetation in forests, desert mountains, canyons, and creeks.

Frogs and salamanders need high levels of moisture in their habitats. The former are usually found directly in or around water, or in the vegetation in humid tropical forests; the latter are easier to locate by lifting rocks and decaying stumps in shaded forests and along the sides of creeks. Most frogs call during their breeding season, providing a convenient way to zero-in on their location.

HELPING OUT

Keeping careful, precise records of your observations can benefit not only you, but others as well. Many organizations and agencies worldwide are now running special conservation programs for reptiles and amphibians. These efforts, which include creating distribution atlases and monitoring amphibian populations, depend on the input of private individuals. If you wish to participate, contact your local herpetological society, or visit some of the websites *(pages 178 to 180)* that deal with these programs to find out who to contact in your area.

Taking a Closer Look

From New Zealand to North America, all the reptiles and amphibians of the world can be divided into eight biological orders. Despite the huge variety in each group, its species share features that distinguish them from the members of other orders.

NEWTS AND SALAMANDERS

Salamanders and newts are sometimes mistaken for lizards, but their moist skin and lack of scales mark them as amphibians rather than reptiles. Like frogs, most species undergo metamorphosis from a larval stage—usually aquatic with gills—to a terrestrial form. Still, there are some that remain entirely aquatic, while others never enter the water at any stage in their life cycle. If aquatic conditions are ideal, some species do not transform, but grow and mature as larger versions of their aquatic form, a process called neoteny or paedomorphosis.

The distinction between salamanders and newts is subtle. Newts tend to have coarser skin and belong to the order Caudata, or salamanders. But while all newts are salamanders, not all salamanders are newts. Regardless, all salamanders are carnivorous, both as larvae and as adults. Food, whether invertebrates or other amphibians, is captured by quick gulps. Larger salamanders will also feed on fish, mammals, or anything else that can fit in their mouth.

Primitive salamanders use external fertilization, although most species employ indirect internal fertilization to compensate for

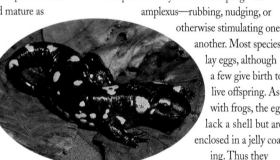

Most salamanders, including the fire salamander (Salamandra salamandra), live in the northern hemisphere.

the male's lack of copulatory organs. In these cases, the male deposits a spermatophore that the female picks up with the lips of her cloaca. Sperm is then released from the spermatophore in the cloaca to fertilize the eggs. This is all dependent on an elaborate courting ritual in order for male and female to recognize and prepare each other, positioning themselves for successful sperm transfer, and the process may involve clasping—or amplexus—rubbing, nudging, or otherwise stimulating one another. Most species lay eggs, although a few give birth to live offspring. As with frogs, the eggs lack a shell but are enclosed in a jelly coating. Thus they must be kept moist.

Although frogs are capable of tissue regeneration only in their larval stage, salamanders retain this ability into adulthood. In some cases, a salamander can wiggle and break off its tail to distract a predator, eventually growing a replacement.

Of the approximately four hundred known species, the smallest lungless salamanders (Plethodontidae) attain a maximum length of one inch (25 mm), while the largest, Chinese giant salamanders (*Andrias davidianus*), can grow as long as six feet (1.8 m).

FROGS AND TOADS

With their frequent mention in folklore, widespread distribution, and unmistakable calls, no group of amphibians is more widely known than frogs and toads. Their ability to colonize habitats ranging from deserts and mountains to prairies and forests has helped to make them highly visible, while the precipitous population decline of many species in the last ten years has alarmed many scientists and called into question the health of planet Earth *(page 60)*.

The general distinction between a frog and a toad, both of which are in the order Anura, is based primarily on appearance. In general, frogs have smooth, moist skin and longer, jumping legs; toads have tough, warty skin to prevent excess water loss and shorter legs used more for short hops or walking and crawling. Despite the differences, all have the same general form: long, muscular hindlegs, often with webbed toes adapted for jumping or swimming, and shorter forelimbs, used to aid in feeding and mating.

The breeding strategies of the approximately four thousand species of anurans are highly diverse. Although most lay eggs and leave them to develop and fend for themselves, some species display remarkable parental care, particularly the males, which may guard nests, carry tadpoles to water, or allow them to develop within their vocal sacs *(page 26)*. Some species lay their eggs on leaves overhanging a water course, where hatching tadpoles fall directly into the water below; others lay them in the water collected in bromeliads. Most eggs hatch into tadpoles, but in many species the larva develops within the egg, with a fully developed froglet emerging directly from the egg.

All frogs, including this red-eyed tree frog (Agalychnis callidryas), undergo metamorphosis (page 24), a transformation from a larval stage to a fully formed adult.

Most people are familiar with frogs through their calls. They are timed between the rest spaces of other calls (which are species-specific) and generally do not overlap, allowing a female to pinpoint her potential mate—thus the "chorus" effect familiar to anyone who has spent a summer evening outdoors in the country.

The role of anurans in the food web is vital. They are an important source of food for fish, reptiles, mammals, birds, and predaceous invertebrates, while their carnivorous diets make them an effective means of insect control. Most species catch their prey with a sticky tongue attached at the front of the mouth, where it can be quickly "flipped" out. Some tongueless species rely on their forelimbs to "scoop" food into their mouth, while others simply leap at their prey with the mouth agape.

CAECILIANS

Caecilians are a unique group of amphibians that live in the tropics. These legless, wormlike animals spend most of their time burrowing, and as a result of their lifestyle, they have very small eyes that may

Caecilians are the least understood order of amphibians, and many people who encounter them mistake them for worms. Shown above is the Central American caecilian (Gymnophis multiplicata).

be concealed under the bones of the skull. With feeble eyesight and no ear openings, they locate and identify their prey by relying on a pair of retractable sensory tentacles between the nostrils and the eyes.

A strong, compact skull with a somewhat pointed snout aids in burrowing, and an underhung jaw helps to capture prey without interfering with tunneling. Their blunt body ends behind the vent or with a very short tail. All caecilians have rings of skin folds, called annuli, that encircle the body. Some species also have bony, fish-like scales buried in the skin of the annuli.

Caecilians employ internal fertilization, which is achieved by a copulatory organ,

called a phallodeum, in the males. Although some species lay eggs, most give birth to live young. Larvae that hatch from eggs laid on moist land or in water are eel-like in appearance, and have gills and a short, finned tail. Metamorphosis occurs in the water, where these features are lost, eyes of the larvae degenerate, and they develop a thicker skin, annuli, sensory tentacles, and a pointed head. In species that give birth to live young, there is no larval stage; the young develop fully within the oviducts of the female.

Caecilians feed occasionally on frogs and lizards, but their diet consists primarily of invertebrates, such as earthworms, encountered during burrowing. Although their skin contains numerous poison glands, they are vulnerable to predators that other amphibians face, including snakes, birds, carnivorous mammals and invertebrates, and other amphibians.

Due to their burrowing lifestyle, little is known about caecilian life history and ecology. There are 156 identified species, ranging in size from 4.5 inches (11 cm) to 60 inches (152 cm). Because caecilians are difficult to find, it is hard for scientists to say with certainty exactly where they exist and whether any of the species are rare or endangered.

LIZARDS

Lizards number approximately four thousand species—more than all the other reptile species put together. They are found on every major land mass outside the cooler regions of the world. Their relatively limited ability to cross mountain ranges and large bodies of water has fostered their evolutionary variety.

Some lizards are legless and may be mistaken for snakes, but they have many discernible identifying features, including external ear openings, a movable eyelid in most species, and, in a few cases, a pineal organ on top of the head that aids in thermoregulation. Species with no legs sometimes have tiny leg buds.

The diversity of locomotory capabilities of lizards makes them unique among the reptiles. Most walk or run, with some species, such as the basilisks of Central America, capable of gaining enough momentum after launching themselves off land that they can run bipedally on water. There are species with ribs that can expand a winglike flap of skin—a patagium—to aid in gliding through treetops, some with toe pads with microscopic suction cups for clinging to flat surfaces, and species with opposable toes on each foot to grip branches. Those that spend their life burrowing—notably a suborder of lizards called Amphisbaenia, or worm lizards—have reduced or no legs, while some lizards have enlarged surfaces on their toes for pushing through sand.

A lizard's tail serves many functions, from helping the animal run or swim to aiding in defense. When threatened, a lizard can whip its tail back and forth or allow it to break off should a predator get a grip on it *(page 41)*. Old World chameleons have a prehensile tail that can grip branches—an ability well suited to their arboreal lifestyle.

Most lizards defend themselves by running away, remaining motionless and inconspicuous, or biting. Two species, the Gila monster (*Heloderma suspectum*) and the Mexican beaded lizard (*Heloderma horridum*), are venomous—the venom flows through grooves in the teeth of the lower jaw while the animal chews its prey. Most lizards are carnivorous, although some are herbivores or omnivores.

As with snakes, the tongue serves as a sensory organ. However, lizards rely mostly on vision, often cuing in on movement.

The vast color spectrum observed among lizards plays an important role in territorial displays, mate selection, and camouflage. Females either lay eggs or give birth to live young.

Chameleons, such as the helmeted chameleon (Chamaeleo hoehnelii) shown above, are able to change the color of their skin to blend in better with the background and thus avoid detection.

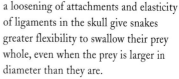

SNAKES

No creature is more easily recognized or universally condemned than the snake. Throughout history, humans have feared and persecuted these legless reptiles. Yet snakes provide a wealth of benefits and many societies today recognize that their carnivorous lifestyle makes them an effective means of pest control, particularly in places where rodents plague human food supplies.

Although there are legless lizards, snakes can be distinguished by the lack of eyelids (the eyes are covered by clear scales) and the absence of ear openings on the side of the head. Because they are incapable of tearing their food into pieces,

a loosening of attachments and elasticity of ligaments in the skull give snakes greater flexibility to swallow their prey whole, even when the prey is larger in diameter than they are.

Many species simply grab their prey with powerful jaws and immediately begin the swallowing process, while others first inject venom. Boas and pythons coil their body around struggling prey, squeezing tighter with every exhalation of the struggling animal until its heart stops beating. Anacondas hold their prey underwater to aid in constricting. A snake's slow metabolism means that they may feed only a few times a year.

Although they have no ears, snakes can detect vibrations through the ground and water. Vision is accomplished with eyes that are covered by transparent scales, rather than protected by movable eyelids, thus giving snakes a non-blinking appearance. Their forked tongue, quickly flickering in and out of the mouth, plays a vital role in detecting scent *(page 45)*.

Most commonly associated with tropical and temperate forests, snakes also have adapted to living underground, in oceans, in deserts, and in alpine meadows—pretty much everywhere outside of the polar regions. Of the twenty-seven hundred known species, the smallest species reaches a maximum length of 4.4 inches (11 cm), while the largest grows more than twenty-eight feet (9 m) long.

Some snakes lay eggs, while species such as the green bush viper (Atheris chloroechis) shown at left give birth to young. Contrary to popular belief, few snakes are venomous.

TURTLES AND TORTOISES

Turtles and tortoises are the most ancient group of living reptiles, little changed in the last 200 million years. They are easily recognized by the hard outer shell, called the carapace, to which the spine and ribs are fused, and a solid plate on the underside, known as the plastron. When threatened, turtles can withdraw into their shell and plastron to protect their head, neck, and limbs. The manner in which they do so leads to their grouping as either hidden-necked turtles (*Cryptodira*), which withdraw their head and neck vertically back into the shell, or side-necked turtles (*Pleurodira*), which tuck their head horizontally into the space between the carapace and plastron. Instead of shedding sheaths of skin during growth like snakes and lizards, turtles shed their scales individually or in small patches, which may appear to peel off their shell. Soft-shelled turtles (*Apalone*) and leatherback turtles (*Dermochelys*) are exceptions. Their carapace consists of a thick, leathery covering rather than bony plates.

The general distinction between a turtle and a tortoise is based on adaptations to the environment. The terms vary worldwide. In North America, tortoises are adapted to life on land and are poor or non-swimmers with large, clubbed, "walking" feet similar in shape to those of an elephant, and often a large, heavy carapace. Turtles have a more stream-lined carapace for swimming and often have webbing between their toes, while terrapin is a term that has been applied to small, aquatic or semi-aquatic turtles other than sea turtles. In England, terrestrial species are called tortoises, freshwater species are terrapins, and marine species are turtles. In Australia, freshwater species are tortoises and marine species are sea turtles.

The Indefatigable Island tortoise (Geochelone nigrita), unique to this island in the Galapagos, is one of the world's biggest tortoises, weighing as much as fifteen hundred pounds (680 kg).

The slow metabolic rate of these animals aids them in going with little or no oxygen for long periods of time, such as when they dive or when they withdraw into their shell for defense. As a result, activity level is slow, as is growth, and they are known to live long lives—occasionally for many decades.

Eggs are laid in a nest that is excavated in the ground and then covered over. Sperm can be stored in females for delayed fertilization during ideal laying conditions. From the moment they are born, hatchlings must fend for themselves and most soon fall prey to predators that include mammals, fish, and other reptiles.

The approximately 250 species in this order have exploited a variety of habitats, from oceans and rivers to forests, grasslands, deserts, and mountains. Their diet is also varied: Some are vegetarians, others scavenge or are carnivores, and still others are omnivores. The smallest species, the speckled cape tortoise (*Homopus signatus*) reaches a maximum weight of five ounces (142 g), while the largest, the leatherback sea turtle, can weigh up to 1,890 pounds (857 kg).

CROCODILES AND ALLIGATORS

This group contains the largest and heaviest of the reptiles, which can grow twenty-three feet (7 m) in length and reach twenty-two hundred pounds (998 kg). Found mainly in the tropics, these semi-aquatic reptiles are distinguished by their large, peglike teeth, powerful tail, and eyes and nostrils set high on the head to remain above the surface of the water while the rest of the body is submerged. All members are carnivores and efficient predators in the aquatic habitats in which they have evolved. Most lie in wait for prey before exploding into action to clamp on it with powerful jaws. Although they are extremely efficient swimmers, crocodiles and alligators tend to be awkward on land when they come ashore to nest. They are capable of short, rapid bursts of movement on land, but usually cannot sustain these sprints for long periods, using them primarily to retreat back to their watery home.

The general feature used to distinguish crocodiles from alligators is the width of the snout—alligators have a wider snout than crocodiles. This isn't always easy to judge, especially when the two are not side-by-side for comparison. Perhaps an easier way to tell them apart is by the teeth. In alligators, the teeth in the lower jaw are not visible when the mouth is closed, whereas the fourth tooth on the lower jaw in crocodiles is visible when the mouth is shut.

Two other members in this grouping are the caiman, alligators in Central and South America, and the gharial, a thin-snouted, fish-eating crocodile of southern Asia. While the diet of most species is mainly fish, any animal small enough to be killed by these reptiles is a potential meal.

All crocodiles lay eggs, which are usually guarded in a nest by the female and sometimes the male. Clutches range from ten to fifty eggs, depending on the species. For some species, clutches produce mainly female offspring at extreme temperatures, while temperatures in the range of eighty-eight to ninety-two degrees Fahrenheit (31 to 33°C) create a more even balance of males and females.

Crocodiles and alligators are in demand for their skin, which is used to make handbags, shoes, and other products for the fashion industry. Over-harvesting drove some species to the brink of extinction during the 1950s and 1960s. Management practices now include rigorously regulated programs that help ensure that the twenty-three species living today will continue to survive.

A black caiman (Melanosuchus niger) feeds on a piranha. Crocodiles are surviving members of the subclass Archosauria, which included dinosaurs.

TUATARA

Tuataras look like lizards, but these reptiles are actually a separate order. Scientists refer to them as "living fossils" since tuataras have changed little since they first roamed the Earth roughly 200 million years ago. About sixty million years ago, tuataras became extinct everywhere except for New Zealand. Once widespread there, the two known species are now limited to about thirty small islands, having been eradicated by rats and other animals introduced from the two main islands in the last few centuries.

The tuatara (Sphenodon) was considered a lizard until the middle of the nineteenth century, when Albert Guenther of the British Museum identified it as the sole survivor of the so-called "beaked-headed" order (Rhynchocephalia), which originated before the age of dinosaurs.

Tuatara means "old spiny back" in the native Maori language. The animals have a series of large, erect spines down the middle of their neck and back. Growing to a length of up to twenty-four inches (61 cm), they have a relatively large head and thick tail in proportion to the rest of their body. The upper jaw is chisel-like, with a row of teeth that overhangs the lower jaw. A second row of teeth runs down the roof of the mouth. The lower jaw has a single row of teeth that fits between the upper rows of teeth when the mouth is closed. These small teeth are not replaced when lost or damaged, and some older tuataras are reduced to chewing their food between smooth jaw bones.

Unlike most lizards, tuataras have no external ear openings; they also have hook-like extensions on some of their ribs and a pineal, or "third" eye, on top of their head—more developed than in lizards—with a retina and rudimentary lens. Its role is still being debated by scientists.

Active mainly at night, tuataras feed predominantly on insects, although they will also eat lizards, birds and their eggs, and other ground-dwelling invertebrates. They spend their day in burrows, which they may have taken over from ground-nesting seabirds—or sometimes share with the birds.

Males are territorial during the late-summer/autumn breeding period, and with no penis, copulation is dependent on direct contact between the pairs' vents, or cloacae. After mating, the partners go their separate ways. On average, females lay up to nineteen eggs about once every four years. Incubation lasts anywhere from twelve to fifteen months, with a temporary cessation in development during the cool winter months. This lengthy breeding process is part of the reason that tuataras have been so vulnerable to extinction. They are now protected in New Zealand.

REPTILES & AMPHIBIANS: A LIFE–ZONE GUIDE

The Biomes &
Their Inhabitants

On the following pages, there are illustrations and descriptions of 162 amphibians and reptiles from around the world. This guide provides a cross-section of species from the eight reptile and amphibian groups: newts and salamanders; frogs and toads; caecilians; lizards; snakes; turtles and tortoises; alligators and crocodiles; and tuataras *(pages 78 to 85)*. Many of the species are included because they are representative of their family or genus, while others have been selected because they are unusual or rare. Taken together, they testify to the remarkable variety found in the world of amphibians and reptiles.

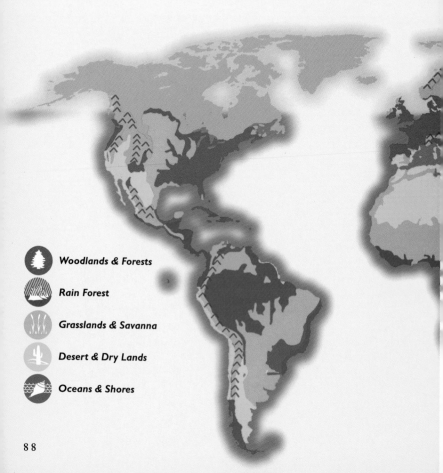

Woodlands & Forests

Rain Forest

Grasslands & Savanna

Desert & Dry Lands

Oceans & Shores

The selection is organized according to biomes: major communities of plants and animals that share similar environmental conditions. Biogeographers organize the world into as many as ten or more biomes, each characterized by a predominant form of vegetation. The five biomes in this guide cover most of the world's land and shorelines: woodlands and forests; rain forest; grasslands and savanna; desert and dry lands; and oceans and shores. This organizational scheme is a useful way to set apart species at a glance. However, assigning a single biome to a species doesn't always tell the whole story since species may live in more than one biome—sometimes many. For example, the common garter snake (*Thamnophis sirtalis*) and the boomslang (*Dispholidus typus*) are found in forests, open areas, wet areas, scrublands, grasslands, and still other environments. Generally, the species that follow are assigned to the biome where they are most often found; other biomes that they may frequent are mentioned in the accompanying descriptions.

Woodlands & Forests

Woodlands and forests are widely distributed across the world's temperate zones. The dominant tree species in these areas include deciduous trees, such as oak, maple, elm, and birch, and evergreen trees, such as spruce and pine. Woodlands and forests occur between approximately 25° and 50° latitude, often with deciduous trees predominating in the lower latitudes, evergreens in the higher, and mixed forests of both occurring in between. Forests are characterized by tall trees that grow close together, forming a near-continuous canopy, while woodlands are made up of much the same tree species but are less dense. In general, these areas are characterized by relatively warm summers and cold winters and a high level of rainfall, ranging from about twenty to eighty inches (50 to 200 cm) a year, with forests receiving more rainfall than woodlands. Defined by their dominant vegetation, biomes also encompass any ponds, rivers, lakes, and other smaller habitats within their boundaries. Many fully aquatic amphibian and reptile species are therefore considered forest and woodland inhabitants.

LIFE IN LAYERS

Woodlands and forests can be divided into different layers: an upper canopy of dominant trees; a lower canopy of smaller trees, shrubs, and plants; and a ground-level layer of leaves, rocks, and soil. Each layer provides a different environment in which amphibians and reptiles can thrive. The deep layer of organic litter on the forest floor provides food, camouflage, protection, and reproductive and hibernation sites for the greatest number of species. For example, most salamanders are often found here, often hiding under rocks and logs. At the same time, certain snakes are more likely to be seen in treetops basking in direct sunlight, and tree frogs and many lizards on the trunks or limbs of the trees.

Forests thrive in areas that have sufficient light, moisture, and soil. They are one of the most abundant and complex biomes found above sea level.

TWO-TOED AMPHIUMA / *Amphiuma means*

This eel-like creature has two pairs of small, almost useless legs, with a pair of toes on each foot, which readily distinguishes it from the other two species of amphiuma in North America: the one-toed and the three-toed. The two-toed amphiuma often makes a small hole in which to hide and wait for prey, such as worms, crayfish, small fish, and frogs, to pass by. Little information is available on the reproductive biology of this species. Most egg masses that have been observed were located on land, although it is believed that the nests were originally constructed in bodies of water that later dried up. To guard the eggs and keep them moist when nests are exposed to the air, females coil themselves around the eggs until they hatch.

Size: 14 to 30 inches (36 to 76 cm)

Range: Coastal plains of southeastern United States

Habitat: Ponds, swamps, streams

Life Cycle: Egg-laying; fifty to two hundred eggs laid in winter

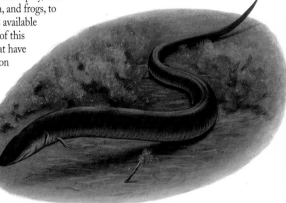

COMMON MUDPUPPY / *Necturus maculosus*

Size: 8 to 19 inches (20 to 49 cm)

Range: Northeastern North America

Habitat: Lakes, ponds, rivers, streams

Life Cycle: Egg-laying; 50 to 120 eggs laid May to June

In the mistaken belief that these large, gilled salamanders bark, they became known as mudpuppies or, in the South, water dogs. While quite abundant, they are rarely seen because they are nocturnal, spending the day in the water hidden under rocks or logs. Anglers often catch these salamanders by accident, and because mudpuppies are considered worthless and even dangerous, they are often discarded on land. Recently groups of mudpuppies have been observed in the water below dams during winter, sometimes on nights as cold as minus twenty-two degrees Fahrenheit (-30°C). It is believed that they are attracted to these spots because of the higher oxygen levels in the water, although it is also possible that these groups are mating or feeding congregations.

91

ALPINE NEWT / *Triturus alpestris*

The blue-gray background color and orange-red belly and throat make this one of the most beautiful newts. Females are easily distinguished from males by the yellow stripe along the lower edge of the tail. Although terrestrial for much of the year, the alpine newt spends most of the summer in water where it mates. Paedomorphosis, a state in which mature amphibians retain gills and other larval characteristics, is common in this species. Like many other newts and salamanders, the alpine newt employs a specialized defense posture when it is threatened, arcing its body so the head and the tail are curved upward to expose the bright red belly. Because of their spectacular colors, this species has been heavily collected for sale as pets.

Size: 3 to 4 inches (8 to 10 cm)

Range: Central and southern Europe

Habitat: Cool, wooded areas with shaded waterways (ponds, lakes, streams)

Life Cycle: Egg-laying; 150 eggs

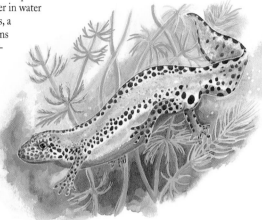

SMOOTH NEWT / *Triturus vulgarus*

Size: 3 to 4 inches (8 to 10 cm)

Range: Northwestern, central, and eastern Europe; western Asia

Habitat: Woodlands, grasslands with ponds

Life Cycle: Egg-laying; two hundred to three hundred eggs laid February to June

Of the eight newts found in Europe, the smooth newt is by far the most common and widespread. It is the only newt that occurs in Ireland and it ranges farther north than any other species, reaching Trondheim in Norway. It is also found in a wide range of habitats, from forests, open woods and meadows to marshes and even gardens. The smooth newt spends more time in terrestrial habitats than most of the other newts in Europe and only returns to ponds to breed. The best way to find it on land is to roll over rocks and logs and sift through the leaf litter.

OLM / *Proteus anguinus*

This is the most easily identifiable salamander in Europe. It is a large, ghostly white, cave-dwelling salamander that is neotenic, meaning it retains the gills. Its arms are tiny, having only three toes on the forelimbs and two on the hindlimbs. The small, rudimentary eyes are completely overgrown with skin, which is why it is often called the blind cave salamander. Relatively little is known about the olm in its wild habitats. Researchers believe that it is a long-lived species, since captives have taken up to fourteen years to reach sexual maturity. There are several similar-looking blind cave salamanders throughout the world, including the Texas blind salamander (*Eurycea rathbuni*).

Size: 10 to 12 inches (25 to 30 cm)

Range: Southeastern Europe

Habitat: Caves with springs, underground streams

Life Cycle: Egg-laying; twelve to seventy eggs

BLUE-SPOTTED SALAMANDER / *Ambystoma laterale*

Size: 3 to 5.5 inches (7.5 to 14 cm)

Range: Northeastern North America

Habitat: Forests

Life Cycle: Egg-laying; 120 to 300 eggs laid April to June

Black with blue flecks, these salamanders are arresting-looking creatures. During the first heavy rains of spring they arrive en masse at ponds in wooded areas. It is not uncommon to see upward of a thousand in one small pond. During the rest of the year, they are quite secretive, usually living underground or under logs and rocks where they feed on worms, snails, and other invertebrates. These salamanders hybridize with three other species of Ambystoma, which has resulted in individuals that are diploid, triploid, or tetraploid (possessing two, three, or four sets of chromosomes). The eggs of triploid females are able to develop without the males' chromosomes. The result is a population of triploid females.

CHINESE GIANT SALAMANDER / *Andrias davidianus*

The Chinese giant salamander—the biggest of all salamanders—lives in cool mountain streams. The species has loose folds of skin that are rich with blood to aid in the absorption of oxygen underwater. In China, the amphibian is widely credited with medical value: It is often eaten for medicinal reasons, with claims that it will improve health and perhaps prevent cancer. Some Chinese even keep the salamander as a pet, believing that it will bring good luck. Chinese giant salamanders are long-lived animals, with some individuals surviving in captivity for more than seventy-five years. In recent years, their numbers have declined because of collection, pollution, and habitat destruction. The species is now protected by law.

Size: 47 to 59 inches (120 to 150 cm)

Range: Southeastern Asia

Habitat: Mountain streams

Life Cycle: Egg-laying

FIRE SALAMANDER / *Salamandra salamandra*

Size: 6 to 10 inches (16 to 25 cm)

Range: Most of Europe, North Africa, Middle East

Habitat: Damp woods with streams and springs

Life Cycle: Live-bearing; ten to thirty well-developed larvae

This is the largest member of its family, but despite its size and abundance, it is seldom seen because of its secretive nature. The salamander usually hides under logs, bark, rocks, or underground in burrows. It is Europe's most widespread species, with many subspecies that are generally distinguished by the variation in their patterns. The striking black and yellow coloring of these creatures is a warning to predators that they are toxic or unpalatable—a trait known as aposematic coloration. Unlike most other salamanders, the fire salamander is almost entirely terrestrial. The females only return to the water body to deposit their larvae and even then they often only submerge the back half of their body.

PACIFIC GIANT SALAMANDER / *Dicamptodon ensatus*

Size: 6.5 to 12 inches (17 to 30 cm)

Range: West coast of United States and south-western Canada

Habitat: Damp forests close to water

Life Cycle: Egg-laying; 70 to 150 eggs laid in May

This beautiful purple-brown salamander is one of the largest land salamanders in North America. It is often found under rocks, logs, and bark in damp forests. When alarmed, it may raise its body off the ground and swing its tail around to lure a predator to the noxious secretions it emits. Sometimes, too, it will make a rattling or growling sound and snap its jaws together. If all else fails to deter a predator, it will bite. Recent research suggests that the Pacific giant salamander is in fact three separate species: one in Idaho (*D. aterrimus*), one in western California (*D. ensatus*), and another that ranges from southwestern Canada to northern California (*D. tenebrosus*).

RED-BACKED SALAMANDER / *Plethodon cinereus*

Recent studies have shown the red-backed salamander to be an extremely abundant forest salamander. While many are seen among leaf litter and under logs or rocks, far more live underground. The red-backed salamander prefers mature forests with deep soil and leaf litter strewn with many rocks and logs. It is fully terrestrial throughout its life cycle. The female lays her eggs in moist cavities, such as the recesses of rotting logs. She then stays with the eggs to guard them from predators and keep them moistened (often by coiling around them). Larval development is completed inside the egg so that on hatching, a tiny replica of an adult emerges.

Size: 2.5 to 5 inches (6.5 to 12.5 cm)

Range: Northeastern North America

Habitat: Forests

Life Cycle: Egg-laying; one to fourteen eggs laid June to July

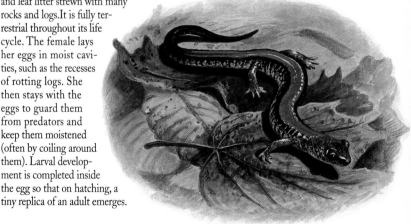

SIBERIAN SALAMANDER / *Salamandrella keyserlingii*

Size: 4 to 5 inches (11 to 13 cm)

Range: Eastern Russia to Siberia, south to Korea

Habitat: Forests

Life Cycle: Egg-laying; fifty to sixty eggs

Although primarily terrestrial, the Siberian salamander breeds in water, where the eggs are attached to sticks, rocks, or vegetation. Unlike most other salamanders, which fertilize internally, Siberian salamanders fertilize their eggs externally after the females have released them. Since this species lives in cool climates, their eggs have a dark pigmentation that absorbs the sun's rays and helps speed up embryo development. The eggs can survive brief periods of freezing temperatures. The adults are even hardier. Some have been known to survive temperatures as low as minus forty-nine degrees Fahrenheit (-45°C) by producing antifreeze-like chemicals in their blood and tissues.

SPRING SALAMANDER / *Gyrinophilus porphyriticus*

Size: 20 to 39 inches (50 to 98 cm)

Range: Appalachian Mountains of eastern North America

Habitat: Springs and damp ground

Life Cycle: Egg-laying; twenty to one hundred eggs laid May to June

These brightly colored salamanders have wedge-shaped heads that enable them to push themselves under or between rocks. There are four subspecies that differ in geographic distribution, colors and patterning. The spring salamander is carnivorous. It eats invertebrates, including slugs, worms, and insect larvae, and it will also dine on smaller adult salamanders.

As a deterrent to mammalian predators, the bright colors of this species warn that its skin secretions are slightly toxic. As with many other salamanders, the number of spring salamanders is declining due to deforestation throughout its range.

GREATER SIREN / *Siren lacertina*

Size: 4 to 8 inches (11 to 21 cm)

Range: Coastal plain of southeastern North America

Habitat: Permanent bodies of water near thick vegetation

Life Cycle: Egg-laying; approximately one hundred eggs laid February to April

This neotenic (larval-like adult) salamander looks like an eel, although it can easily be distinguished by its external gills and reduced forelimbs. Sirens are nocturnal and come out at night to feed primarily on snails. They spend the day in ponds or other bodies of water, hiding in burrows dug at the bottom with their shovel-like head. If the pond dries up, they dig deeper into the pond bottom, shedding their outer layer of skin, which acts like a cocoon, and then estivating until heavy rains return. They are capable of spending years in this reduced metabolic state.

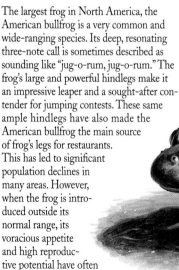

AMERICAN BULLFROG / *Rana catesbeiana*

The largest frog in North America, the American bullfrog is a very common and wide-ranging species. Its deep, resonating three-note call is sometimes described as sounding like "jug-o-rum, jug-o-rum." The frog's large and powerful hindlegs make it an impressive leaper and a sought-after contender for jumping contests. These same ample hindlegs have also made the American bullfrog the main source of frog's legs for restaurants. This has led to significant population declines in many areas. However, when the frog is introduced outside its normal range, its voracious appetite and high reproductive potential have often made it an abundant pest.

Size: 3.5 to 8 inches (9 to 20 cm)

Range: Across North America, excluding prairies

Habitat: Pond, lakes, slow-moving rivers

Life Cycle: Egg-laying; 1,000 to 25,000 eggs laid February to August

AFRICAN CLAWED FROG / *Xenopus laevis*

The Greek word *xenopus* means "unusual foot," a reference to the claws that set these frogs apart from most other species. In the 1930s the African clawed frog gained prominence in the medical world when it began to be used in pregnancy testing: It was discovered that when urine from a pregnant woman is injected under the skin of these frogs, the males discharge sperm and the females lay eggs. This was a quicker and more humane approach than earlier pregnancy testing methods that required the killing of rabbits or mice. The frogs are both prolific and insatiably carnivorous. As a result, after they were introduced to habitats in southwestern North America, native frog species declined markedly.

Size: 2 to 5.5 inches (5 to 14 cm)

Range: Southern half of Africa, introduced into southwestern North America

Habitat: Rivers, ponds

Life Cycle: Egg-laying; two thousand eggs laid November to June

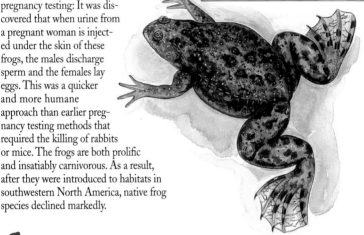

EUROPEAN COMMON FROG / *Rana temporaria*

Size: 3 to 4 inches (7 to 10 cm)

Range: Most of Europe and Asia to Japan, excluding southern regions

Habitat: Forests, fields

Life Cycle: Egg-laying; two thousand to four thousand eggs laid March to June

Living up to its name, the European common frog is one of the most widespread frogs in Europe. The species can thrive in many different habitats as long as there is a body of water close by. Because of its wide range, its coloration is highly variable, ranging from browns and grays to olives and yellows and even pinks. As communal breeders, these frogs often produce shared egg clusters that contain many thousands of eggs. Researchers have found that these large clusters cool down less quickly at night. This protects the embryos from freezing and allows them to develop around the clock. Following metamorphosis, it is not unusual to see thousands of froglets in the vicinity of a breeding pond.

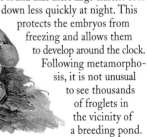

DARWIN'S FROG / *Rhinoderma darwinii*

Size: 1 to 1.2 inches (2.5 to 3 cm)

Range: Southern Argentina and Chile

Habitat: Beech forests

Life Cycle: Egg-laying; twenty to thirty eggs laid throughout year, most often December to March

Named after the great naturalist Charles Darwin, this frog is distinguished by a long snoutlike extension of skin. The unusual shape of its head aids in camouflage by giving this species a harder-to-recognize, or cryptic, profile. A remarkable characteristic of the Darwin's frog is a reproductive strategy called mouth brooding, which is seen in only one other related species. After the females lay the eggs, the males watch over them. When the larvae begin to wriggle around, indicating that the eggs are close to hatching, the males pick up the eggs with their tongues. The eggs slide through an opening into their vocal sac. Once the larvae have gone through metamorphosis, they emerge from the mouth as tiny froglets.

GOLD FROG / *Brachycephalus ephippium*

This bright gold frog is also known as the saddle-backed toad, a reference to the bony, cross-shaped shield, or saddle, fused to its back. Researchers believe the frog blocks the entrance to its burrow with the shield to keep the burrow moist and prevent predators from entering. Because water is limited in its habitat, the species buries its eggs in the ground to keep them moist.

The gold frog has just two fingers on its hands and three toes on its feet. Because of these and other characteristics, experts have recently removed the gold frog from the family Bufonidae, so-called "true toads," and placed it in the family Brachycephalidae. This family includes the world's smallest toad, *Psyllophryne didactyla*, which as an adult measures just about a half inch (1 cm) in length.

Size: 0.5 to 1 inch (1.6 to 2.2 cm)

Range: Southeastern Brazil

Habitat: Leaf litter of forest floor

Life Cycle: Egg-laying

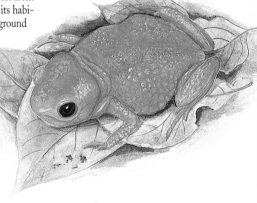

99

GREENHOUSE FROG / *Eleutherodactylus planirostris*

Recently introduced to the United States, this small frog is often found in greenhouses and gardens under flower pots and in similar moist spots—beneath logs, boards, and leaf litter. Of the roughly 450 species of frogs in its genus, all but one go through metamorphosis while still in the egg. Once they hatch, the tiny froglets that emerge are only 0.2 inch (0.5 cm) long and look like miniature, tailed versions of adults. Soon the tail is absorbed by the body and the frog begins to feed on a wide range of insects, including ants, beetles, and cockroaches. The high-pitched croaking of the greenhouse frog is often mistaken as a bird call.

Size: 0.8 to 1.2 inches (2 to 3 cm)

Range: West Indies, introduced into south-eastern United States

Habitat: Forested areas, open areas especially around human developments

Life Cycle: Egg-laying; ten to twenty-six eggs laid May to September

HAMILTON'S FROG / *Leiopelma hamiltonii*

Size: 1.5 to 2 inches (3.5 to 5 cm)

Range: Stephens Island, Maud Island in New Zealand

Habitat: Humid forests

Life Cycle: Egg-laying; one to twenty-two eggs

This extremely rare frog is found on only two islands in New Zealand. Unlike most frogs, which have a tongue attached at the front of the mouth, the Hamilton's frog has a tongue secured at the back. This prevents the frog from flicking out its tongue to catch food. Instead, it lunges at prey with its mouth agape and stuffs in the food with its front legs. The eggs of this species are laid on land, where they are guarded and kept moist by the male. When they hatch as partially developed, tiny-tailed froglets, the young climb onto the male's back. After about a month, the 0.4-inch (1-cm) -long froglets are fully developed and hop off.

TABLE MOUNTAIN GHOST FROG / *Heleophryne rosei*

Size: 2 to 2.5 inches (5 to 6.5 cm)

Range: Table Mountain in South Africa

Habitat: Mountain streams in forests

Life Cycle: Egg-laying; one hundred to two hundred eggs

Limited to the Table Mountain region in South Africa, this species inhabits cold, fast-flowing streams. There is nothing "ghostly" about this frog, other than the fact that the species may have been first discovered in a local formation called Skeleton Gorge. These frogs are well adapted to their watery habitat. Large suctionlike discs on their toes and small hooks along the skin of their forearms and toes help adults maneuver on slippery rocks. The eggs cling to the rocks and the tadpoles that emerge have a streamlined wedge shape, which makes them unique among tadpoles. This adaptation, along with large sucking mouth discs, prevents the tadpoles from being pulled from the algae-covered rocks where they feed.

TAILED FROG / *Ascaphus truei*

One of a primitive group of frogs related to the *Leiopelma* of New Zealand, the tailed frog has adapted well to the fast-moving waters of its habitat. For example, the tail referred to in its name (seen only on the males) is in fact a copulatory organ that allows the male to pass sperm directly into the body of the female. This is a big advantage in turbulent water where sperm would be washed away during external fertilization. The tadpoles avoid being pulled downstream by clamping onto rocks with their strong disc-shaped mouth.

Size: 1 to 2 inches (2.5 to 5 cm)

Range: Northwestern United States, southwestern Canada

Habitat: Rocky, cold forest streams

Life Cycle: Egg-laying; thirty to fifty eggs laid May to July

WOOD FROG / *Rana sylvatica*

Wood frogs hibernate in temperatures well below freezing, with the water in their body actually freezing solid. Like the gray tree frog *(page 105)*, the wood frog survives these periods with the aid of antifreeze compounds that protect cells that have been drained of water. Water from cells is stored in bodily spaces where it can freeze without causing damage. This ability allows the wood frog to live farther north than any other amphibian or reptile in North America. The wood frog mates for just a few days every year, right after the snow melts. Since competition for mates is high and conditions are crowded, males can often be observed attempting to mate with other males or even inanimate objects.

Size: 1.5 to 3.5 inches (4 to 9 cm)

Range: Northeastern United States, most of Canada

Habitat: Wooded areas

Life Cycle: Egg-laying; one thousand to three thousand eggs laid April to June

COMMON SPADEFOOT / *Pelobates fuscus*

This nocturnal burrowing toad is capable of quickly digging a hole by using the small projections on its hind foot as a shovel—hence its common name. It is also referred to as the garlic toad because of the odor it emits when disturbed. It may also try to fend off predators by raising itself up high on its legs, puffing itself up, and wailing loudly. Or, it may jump at its attacker with its mouth open. Perhaps the most startling thing about this toad is the size of its tadpoles, by far the biggest of any other European species. The largest ones are close to seven inches (18 cm) long.

Size: 2.5 to 3.5 inches (6.5 to 9 cm)

Range: Central and eastern Europe, western Asia

Habitat: Areas with sandy soil

Life Cycle: Egg-laying; eggs laid April to May

AMERICAN TOAD / *Bufo americanus*

One of the most terrestrial of amphibians, the American toad is often found far from water and is a familiar sight from forests to fields to backyards. Its skin contains glands with a poisonous milky fluid that keeps most predators at bay. During breeding season, the males serenade females with a musical trill that lasts as long as thirty seconds at a time. To make their calls stand out among the competing chorus, males will vary the pitch of their call from their neighbors'. Temperature also affects the mating call: The lower the temperature, the longer the trill.

Size: 2.5 to 4 inches (6.5 to 11 cm)

Range: Eastern North America from central Quebec to Louisiana

Habitat: Wide-ranging; from thick forests to meadows, dunes, swamps

Life Cycle: Egg-laying; four thousand to twelve thousand eggs laid April to July

EUROPEAN COMMON TOAD / *Bufo bufo*

Size: 5 to 7 inches (12 to 18 cm)

Range: Europe, Asia

Habitat: Wooded areas, fields, gardens

Life Cycle: Egg-laying; two thousand to five thousand eggs laid April to May

This is the biggest European toad. Its large size, bitter skin secretions, and defensive tactics of rising up on its legs, puffing up, and head butting have ensured that it has few predators—although the abundant tadpoles are eaten by numerous snakes. The European common toad has often been studied for its remarkable homing abilities. One individual released about two miles (3 km) from its home returned to the exact spot where it was captured. In accomplishing such journeys, these toads rely primarily on smell.

FIRE-BELLIED TOAD / *Bombina bombina*

This toad has a red, speckled belly, but is well camouflaged when seen from above. Only if threatened will it rise up and show off its bright underside—a reminder to would-be predators that the species produces a mildly toxic skin secretion. Its triangular or heart-shaped pupils set the fire-bellied toad apart from other frogs and toads, most of which have horizontal, slit-shaped pupils. In German, this species is known as *unke*, a generic word for toad and also a specific reference to the call of the fire-bellied toad, which sounds something like "unk-unk."

Size: 1.5 to 2 inches (4 to 5 cm)

Range: Central and eastern Europe

Habitat: Ponds, slow-moving water in wooded areas and meadows

Life Cycle: Egg-laying; twenty to fifty eggs laid April to July

MIDWIFE TOAD / *Alytes obstetricans*

The common name of this toad refers to its unusual reproductive behavior. Most toads mate in water, but this species mates on land. The male stimulates the female to extend her hindlegs, which makes a receptacle where the male can fertilize the eggs as they are deposited. The male then wraps the string of eggs around his hindlegs and carries them away. When the eggs are close to hatching, after about three weeks, he takes them to water. The young then hatch as advanced tadpoles, living in the water for approximately a year before metamorphosing into adult frogs. The midwife toad is also known as the bell toad because of its musical, bell-like croak.

Size: 1.8 to 2.4 inches (4.5 to 6 cm)

Range: Southwestern and central Europe

Habitat: Wooded hills

Life Cycle: Egg-laying; twenty to sixty eggs laid April to August

GRAY TREE FROG / *Hyla versicolor*

Size: 1.2 to 2.4 inches (3 to 6 cm)

Range: Eastern North America

Habitat: Forests

Life Cycle: Egg-laying; fifty to sixty eggs laid April to July

With skin that mimics the look of lichen-covered bark and the capability of turning from gray to green, this large tree frog enjoys excellent camouflage. Bright orange patches hidden in the folds of the hindlegs are exposed when the frog jumps. This is thought to confuse or startle predators, giving time for escape. An amazing characteristic of this frog—as well as some of its relatives, such as the wood frog *(page 102)*—is that parts of its body freeze solid in winter. As temperatures drop, water is pumped from cells and stored in bodily spaces between cells. There it can freeze without causing cells to burst. Meanwhile, the production of antifreeze compounds containing glycerol help prevent cells themselves from freezing.

GREEN ANOLE / *Anolis carolinensis*

The green anole is capable of changing colors, depending on lighting, temperature, and its emotional status. This ability has earned the small lizard the name "chameleon," a misnomer since the only true chameleons are the ones that live in the Old World. The green anole is an arboreal lizard that can be found in just about any habitat type within its range. Its widespread abundance makes it

Size: 5 to 8 inches (12.5 to 20 cm)

Range: South, central, eastern North America

Habitat: Forests, open areas

Life Cycle: Egg-laying; one to two eggs laid March to September

one of the most familiar lizards in North America and thousands are sold each year in the pet trade. The males' habit of displaying for territory and for females by bobbing up and down and spreading out their bright pink throat fan makes this a fascinating lizard to own and observe.

MARBLED GECKO / *Phyllodactylus marmoratus*

Size: 5 to 6 inches (13 to 15 cm)

Range: Southern Australia

Habitat: Cool, wet forests

Life Cycle: Egg-laying; one to two eggs

Named for its patterned skin, the marbled gecko features broad, leaflike clinging pads on its toes, which enable it to climb in trees. Because it has been out-competed by a group of other geckos in the genus *Gehydra*, this species has been forced into cooler, wetter forested areas, where it has developed a tolerance for the cold. The female lays eggs slightly larger than that of other geckos, which enables hatchlings to better survive their harsher environment. The eggs are usually placed under rocks or are hidden in debris.

MEDITERRANEAN GECKO / *Hemidactylus turcicus*

Widely distributed around the Mediterranean Sea, this species was once better known as the Turkish gecko, hence the scientific name *H. turcicus*. Geckos are one of the few reptiles with well-developed vocal abilities, and the Mediterranean gecko is among the loudest of the gecko species. Its call—somewhere between a mouselike squeak and a sort of mewing sound—is used to defend territory, especially during the breeding season, and also to startle predators. Highly adaptable, the Mediterranean gecko has successfully colonized many of the regions where it has been introduced. It is often seen hunting for insects around lights at night. Like most geckos, it is an extremely adept climber and can even walk across ceilings.

Size: 3.5 to 5.5 inches (9 to 14 cm)

Range: Southern Europe, southwestern Asia, northern Africa, introduced into North and Central America

Habitat: Many habitats, from woodlands to human-inhabited areas

Life Cycle: Egg-laying; one to two eggs per clutch, four to five clutches laid April to August

WILLIAM'S GECKO / *Diplodactylus williamsii*

Size: 3.5 to 4.3 inches (9 to 11 cm)

Range: Northeastern, central-eastern Australia

Habitat: Open woodlands

Life Cycle: Egg-laying; one to two eggs

With its large eyes, specially ridged toes for gripping, and a prehensile tail, the William's gecko is well-equipped for foraging along tree trunks at night. Also called the spiny-tailed gecko, it employs an unusual defensive technique, shooting a sticky cobweblike substance from its spines to distract its attackers. Like most geckos, the William's gecko is a master in the art of tail loss to free itself from the grasp of a hungry predator. It can break off its tail just above the point of contact, sacrificing only a small part of the appendage, which is normally used to store fat.

FIJI BANDED IGUANA / *Brachylophus fasciatus*

Size: 20 to 32 inches (50 to 80 cm)

Range: Fiji, Tonga, associated islands in south Pacific Ocean

Habitat: Forests, especially wet lowlands

Life Cycle: Egg-laying, three to six eggs laid December to March

Little is known about this rare iguana. It is semi-arboreal, usually found in Tahitian chestnut or ivy trees. An omnivorous species, it eats insects, leaves, and flowers. When dining on leaves or flowers, it holds onto the food with its front feet while grasping the branch with its hind feet and balancing with its long tail. The species has been eliminated from many of the islands it once inhabited; its eggs and young fell prey to the mongoose, which was introduced to control rat populations. The continued survival of the Fiji banded iguana is uncertain.

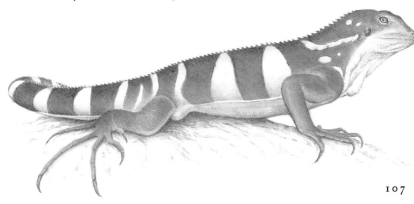

FLORIDA WORM LIZARD / *Rhineura floridana*

Sometimes called the Florida worm snake, this species is neither a snake nor a full-fledged lizard. It is an amphisbaenid—the only member of the suborder that occurs in the United States. Its color and appearance, along with the rings of scales that encircle its body, give it the look of an earthworm. Like the earthworm, it is fossorial—that is, adapted to digging. The creature does not have limbs, external ear openings, or external eyes (although there are remnants hidden under the skin). Its jaws are countersunk to allow for burrowing. The worm lizard is seldom seen, but it often comes to the surface during and immediately after a heavy rain to escape its flooded burrow.

Size: 7 to 11 inches (18 to 28 cm)

Range: Most of Florida, along Gulf Coast, Texas in United States

Habitat: Fossorial in sandy areas

Life Cycle: Egg-laying; one to three eggs laid June to July

FRILLED LIZARD / *Chlamydosaurus kingii*

Size: 18 to 37 inches (45 to 95 cm)

Range: Forests, scrublands

Habitat: Southern New Guinea to northern Australia

Life Cycle: Egg-laying; four to thirteen eggs

This lizard gets its name from the pleated skin around its neck, which can be erected to startle attackers. The loose skin is attached to the neck by bones that give it structural support. The lizard may also try to deter predators by opening its mouth and exposing the bright red lining. If all else fails, it will rise up on its hindlegs and run toward its foe. The impressive display is all show: The frilled lizard is harmless. It spends most of its time in the trees, occasionally coming to the ground to forage on insects and small vertebrates.

GRAY BURROWING LIZARD / *Blanus cinereus*

Size: 8 to 12 inches (20 to 30 cm)

Range: Spain, Portugal, northwestern Africa

Habitat: Woodlands with moist, sandy soil

Life Cycle: Probably egg-laying

Like the Florida worm lizard *(page opposite)*, the gray burrowing lizard belongs to the suborder of lizards called *Amphisbaenia*, otherwise known as worm lizards. Very little is known about the gray burrowing lizard, which lives a secretive digging life. It is most often encountered by people who are turning logs or stones, or digging in the soil. Its cylindrical body, ringlike grooves, and lack of limbs make it look more like a large earthworm than anything else. It is an opportunistic feeder, eating many types of insects as well as other invertebrates and small vertebrates.

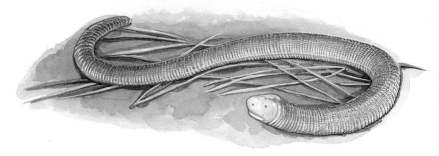

NORTHERN ALLIGATOR LIZARD / *Elgaria coeruleus*

Size: 9 to 13 inches (22 to 33 cm)

Range: Southwestern Canada, northwestern United States

Habitat: Forests, woodlands, grassy areas

Life Cycle: Live-bearing; two to fifteen young born June to September

With its short legs and thick, tight-fitting scales, the northern alligator lizard drags its belly on the ground as it walks, moving its body in a swinging, side-to-side fashion much as alligators do. The lizard's tail is prehensile, used for climbing and hanging onto branches when it makes arboreal hunting forays. Most of the time it hides under rocks, logs, and bark. Its diet includes small invertebrates such as spiders, ticks, and beetles. When it is threatened, the northern alligator lizard will hiss and open its mouth wide. One should heed this warning: This lizard will bite if given the opportunity.

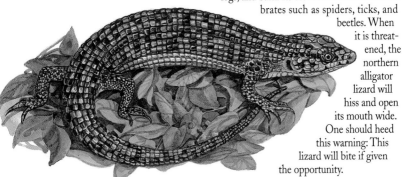

VIVIPAROUS LIZARD / *Lacerta vivipara*

Size: 4 to 7 inches (11 to 18 cm)

Range: Most of northern and central Europe through Asia

Habitat: Highly variable, from sand dunes to forest edges

Life Cycle: Live-bearing; five to eight young born June to September

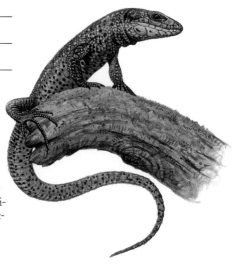

The ground-dwelling viviparous lizard has the largest range of any reptile in the world. It is often referred to as the common lizard because it is found in such a diversity of habitats, making its home in ditches, bogs, meadows, gardens, or even in alpine areas. Although the viviparous lizard is usually live-bearing, it also may lay eggs in some parts of its range. This is possible because it utilizes a method of reproduction referred to as ovoviviparity, in which the embryos are retained inside the female, but receive their nutrients from a yolk sac rather than a placenta.

BLUE-TONGUED SKINK / *Tiliqua scincoides*

Size: 16 to 24 inches (40 to 60 cm)

Range: Northern and eastern Australia, associated islands

Habitat: Woodlands, forests, grasslands

Life Cycle: Live-bearing; ten to twenty young

When threatened, this large fleshy skink rises up in a defensive display and opens its mouth wide to show off its big blue tongue and brilliant red mouth. There are many similar species and subspecies of blue-tongued skinks, each easily distinguished by color pattern and geographic location. All are diurnal, heat-loving lizards that wait for warm temperatures before emerging from their hiding places under logs and leaf litter. This lizard is often seen basking in the sun, raising its body temperature in preparation for the day's activities. A higher body temperature also helps it digest its diet of invertebrates, flowers, and fruits. The blue-tongued skinks are among the largest skinks in the world.

FIVE-LINED SKINK / *Eumeces fasciatus*

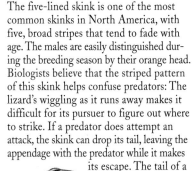

Size: 5 to 8 inches (12 to 20 cm)

Range: Eastern North America

Habitat: Humid forests, edges of hardwood forests, gardens

Life Cycle: Egg-laying: four to fifteen eggs laid May to June

The five-lined skink is one of the most common skinks in North America, with five, broad stripes that tend to fade with age. The males are easily distinguished during the breeding season by their orange head. Biologists believe that the striped pattern of this skink helps confuse predators: The lizard's wiggling as it runs away makes it difficult for its pursuer to figure out where to strike. If a predator does attempt an attack, the skink can drop its tail, leaving the appendage with the predator while it makes its escape. The tail of a juvenile is a brilliant blue, which draws attackers to the least vital part of the skink's body, further improving the young lizard's chance of survival.

SLOWORM / *Anguis fragilis*

This snakelike creature is sometimes known as the blindworm, although it is neither blind nor a worm. Perhaps more surprising to the casual observer, the slowworm is not a snake either, but a lizard. On close inspection, several features distinguish the slowworm from a snake. These include tiny ear cavities, which are sometimes covered, movable eyelids, and a lizardlike skull. The slowworm has a very fragile tail that often snaps off, hence the Latin name *Anguis fragilis*, or "brittle snake." Females retain dark vertebral stripes through adulthood. A less common blue-spotted form is found in some parts of the range (with both males and females displaying spots).

Size: 14 to 21 inches (35 to 54 cm)

Range: Europe, northern Africa, western Asia

Habitat: Open areas, fields, grassy meadows

Life Cycle: Live-bearing; three to twenty-six young born August to September

BOOMSLANG / *Dispholidus typus*

Size: 47 to 63 inches (120 to 160 cm)

Range: Southern Africa

Habitat: Open woodlands

Life Cycle: Egg-laying; up to twenty-five eggs laid in early summer

Named after the Afrikaan word for tree snake, the boomslang is a diurnal species that hunts chameleons and small birds. It relies on its specially designed ventral scales to move through the trees stealthily and its binocular vision to seek out prey. Although the females are a drab olive, the males may be powdery blue, bright green, or mottled with black and gold. This relatively large venomous snake is shy, but when threatened or harassed it will inflate its neck, exposing black skin, and may strike. Its venom is highly toxic and causes hemorrhaging and sometimes death.

RUBBER BOA / *Charina bottae*

The rubber boa is one of only two species of boas found in the United States. It is named for its patternless brown-olive skin, which looks and feels somewhat rubbery. Its blunt tail and a clever defensive technique have earned it another name: the two-headed snake. When threatened, the snake coils its body around its head for protection, then confuses predators by mimicking head movements with its tail. Like many other snakes, it also produces a foul-smelling musk to deter predators. Because it is a burrower, the rubber boa is usually found in areas with loose soil or abundant leaf litter. It feeds on invertebrates, small mammals, and birds, which it subdues by constriction.

Size: 14 to 33.5 inches (35 to 85 cm)

Range: Northwestern United States

Habitat: Forested regions

Life Cycle: Live-bearing; two to eight young born August to November

KING COBRA / *Ophiophagus hannah*

The king cobra is the largest venomous snake in the world. Despite the common impression of cobras as snakes that spend their life with the fore part of their body off the ground and sport a flattened neck, they normally look just like other snakes. But when a cobra is threatened, it will rear up and spread out its specially elongated ribs to flatten out the skin, forming its distinctive "hood." In this posture, the king cobra may stand as much as sixty inches (152 cm) high, tall enough to easily look an adult human in the eyes. Fortunately, this giant snake tends to slither away when disturbed.

Size:	157.5 to 216.5 inches (400 to 550 cm)
Range:	Southeastern Asia, nearby islands
Habitat:	Forests, often close to streams
Life Cycle:	Egg laying; twenty-one to forty eggs

AESCULAPIAN SNAKE / *Elaphe longissima*

Size:	39 to 79 inches (100 to 200 cm)
Range:	Central and southern Europe
Habitat:	Open woodlands
Life Cycle:	Egg-laying; five to twenty eggs laid in July

The ability of snakes to shed their skin and emerge healthier led the ancient Greeks to associate them with healing and reincarnation. The aesculapian snake, a species regarded as sacred, was named after the Greek god of medicine, Aesculapius, who carried a staff with a snake wound around it. Because of the snake's religious significance, it was carried outside of its native habitat. Remnant populations remain in Germany and Switzerland in places where Roman spas existed. This species has an elaborate mating dance: Male and female begin by facing each other with their latter third raised in the air. They then move around and twist their raised anterior parts together.

CAT-EYED SNAKE / *Leptodeira septentrionalis*

Size: 24 to 43 inches (60 to 110 cm)

Range: Southern Texas through Central America to Peru

Habitat: Lowland forests

Life Cycle: Egg-laying, six to twelve eggs

This arboreal, nocturnal snake has vertical pupils similar to those of a cat, a physiological adaptation that improves night vision. Its species name, *septentrionalis*, is from the Latin word for northern; no other member of *Leptodeira* lives so far north. The cat-eyed snake is usually found in areas where there is an abundance of frogs, its primary prey, although it will also feed on small lizards and snakes. *L. septentrionalis* belongs in the group known as rear-fanged snakes because its fangs are at the back of its mouth. It must get a good grip on its prey before it can deliver its venom.

EASTERN HOG-NOSE SNAKE / *Heterodon platirhinos*

This stout-bodied snake is easily identified by its upturned nose, which it uses to burrow in sandy soils when foraging for toads, its main food source. Hog-nose snakes are well known for a defense behavior that has led them to be erroneously called blow vipers, hiss adders, or puff adders. If molested, they spread the skin on their head and neck, creating a hood similar to a cobra's, and hiss loudly. If this doesn't scare away the intruder, they will play dead by lying coiled on their back, mouth open, with the tongue hanging out.

Size: 20 to 33 inches (51 to 84 cm)

Range: Eastern North America

Habitat: Thinly wooded areas with sandy soil

Life Cycle: Egg-laying; four to sixty-one eggs laid June to July

EGG-EATING SNAKE / *Dasypeltis scabra*

As its name suggests, this species is a highly-specialized hunter and eater of eggs, particularly birds' eggs. Thanks to a detachable-jaw mechanism, the egg-eating snake is capable of eating an egg that is four to five times bigger than its head. Once in the mouth, the egg is punctured with a pointy extension of a vertebrae that sticks out into the throat, then it is crushed and swallowed. Later the shell is regurgitated in a single compacted piece. This species is non-venomous and has very few teeth. To defend itself from predators, it mimics the look and behavior of vipers in its habitat, rubbing its scales together to make a hissing noise and striking with a gaping mouth.

Size: 22 to 35 inches (55 to 90 cm)

Range: Africa south of Sahara Desert

Habitat: Forest edges, open woodlands, grasslands

Life Cycle: Egg-laying; sixteen to twenty-three eggs laid December to March

COMMON GARTER SNAKE / *Thamnophis sirtalis*

With twelve subspecies, the garter snake is probably North America's best known and most widely distributed snake. It is also the continent's most northerly-occurring snake species, with a range that extends to about 67°N latitude. The garter hates to sleep alone. In some areas, more than ten thousand snakes gather to hibernate communally. When threatened or handled, the garter produces a foul-smelling musk from its cloaca and rubs the substance over its body. It will also bite in self-defense. The snake's common name comes from its resemblance to the striped elastic garters that fashionable men once used to hold up their socks.

Size: 18 to 39 inches (45 to 100 cm)

Range: Most of North America

Habitat: Forests to fields

Life Cycle: Live-bearing; seven to eighty-five young born June to August

GRASS SNAKE / *Natrix natrix*

The colors and patterns of the grass snake vary widely, but the species is easily identified by its distinctive orange-to-white neck collar. Its Latin name, *Natrix*, means water, and this is where the snake is most often seen, hunting for frogs, salamanders, newts, and fish. The grass snake rarely bites, but it boasts an impressive defensive display. When threatened, it will repeatedly puff up and deflate its body, hiss loudly, and make fake strikes (it keeps its mouth closed). It will also excrete a foul-smelling liquid from its vent. If all else fails, it may attempt to pretend that it is dead by going limp, rolling onto its back, opening its mouth, and letting its tongue hang out.

Size:	27.5 to 59 inches (70 to 150 cm)
Range:	Most of Europe, northwest Africa, western Asia
Habitat:	Thick vegetation close to water
Life Cycle:	Egg-laying; eleven to twenty-five eggs laid June to September

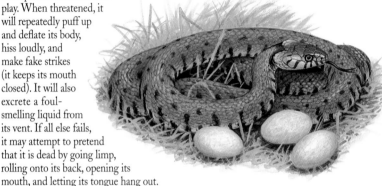

MANDARIN RATSNAKE / *Elaphe mandarina*

Size:	27.5 to 51 inches (70 to 130 cm)
Range:	Southeastern Asia
Habitat:	Sparsely forested upland slopes
Life Cycle:	Egg-laying; three to eight eggs

With its arresting yellow and black markings, the Mandarin ratsnake is one of the most beautiful snakes in the world. Despite its brilliant coloration, it is well camouflaged in its natural environment of forest leaf litter in the dappled sun. In addition to its regular diet of small rodents, the Mandarin ratsnake also eats birds and eggs. It is particularly fond of nestlings, plucking them out of their nest and killing them by constriction before it swallows them whole. The nocturnal snake leaves the forest in the evening and can often be found foraging around agricultural areas, especially rice fields, where there is an abundance of small rodents.

BANDED KRAIT / *Bungarus fasciatus*

The banded krait's brilliant yellow and dark bands and its large size (it is the largest of the kraits) give it a formidable presence. With a bite that releases five times the venom needed to kill an adult human, this snake should never be handled. While very timid, it is known to bite when repeatedly disturbed or cornered. The banded krait most often eats other snakes, both venomous and non-venomous, although when these are scarce it feeds on lizards or small mammals. The females show a degree of parental care by excavating a shallow depression for a nest, which is usually hidden by debris, and remaining with the eggs to protect them from predators.

Size: 47 to 79 inches (120 to 200 cm)

Range: Southeastern Asia

Habitat: Forest edges, grassy areas, near water

Life Cycle: Egg-laying; six to ten eggs

SLIDER / *Trachemys scripta*

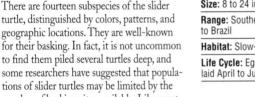

There are fourteen subspecies of the slider turtle, distinguished by colors, patterns, and geographic locations. They are well-known for their basking. In fact, it is not uncommon to find them piled several turtles deep, and some researchers have suggested that populations of slider turtles may be limited by the number of basking sites available. Like most young turtles, immature sliders are predominantly carnivorous, while older individuals are omnivorous and eat a large amount of vegetation. Old males and large females are often very difficult to identify because they lose their characteristic patternings and appear to be predominantly black in color.

Size: 8 to 24 inches (20 to 60 cm)

Range: Southeastern and central United States to Brazil

Habitat: Slow-moving freshwater habitats

Life Cycle: Egg-laying; two to twenty-five eggs laid April to July

AFRICAN SOFT-SHELLED TURTLE / *Trionyx triunguis*

As the common names suggests, this turtle is soft-shelled and lacks the horny plates that are characteristic of most turtles. Its wide distribution traverses many biomes. But as a totally aquatic turtle, leaving the water only to bask and nest, it is always found in or around a waterway. Its flattened, tapered body facilitates swimming and also enables the turtle to bury itself in the bottom of the river, where it waits in hiding for a fish, a frog, or some invertebrate to come by. Most of its life is spent underwater, so the African soft-shelled turtle is capable of breathing by using its skin and a pharynx loaded with extra blood vessels to draw oxygen from water.

Size: 16 to 29.5 inches (40 to 75 cm)

Range: Africa, except for northwest and extreme south, southwest Asia

Habitat: Ponds, lakes, slow-moving rivers or streams, occasionally in ocean

Life Cycle: Egg-laying; twenty-five to one hundred eggs laid March to July

BIG-HEADED TURTLE / *Plastysternon megacephalum*

Size: Up to 7 inches (18 cm)

Range: Southern China to northern and central Indochina

Habitat: Mountain streams with rocky bottoms

Life Cycle: Egg-laying; one to two eggs

This is the only species in the family Platysternidae, although five subspecies are recognized, varying in coloration, patterns, and some structural features. With a head too big to fit inside its shell, this turtle has developed a shieldlike protective plate on top of its head. The big-headed turtle is seldom seen basking. Instead, it burrows into the gravel or hides under rocks in the stream bed by day, emerging at night to feed mainly on fish and invertebrates. Carnivorous and having a large head and mouth, it is well equipped to deliver a serious bite to anyone who comes too close.

The greatest threat to its survival is collection for the pet trade.

BOG TURTLE / *Clemmys muhlenbergii*

This small turtle is easily identified by the bright orange-yellow markings on the sides of its head. Its preferred habitat, a sphagnum bog, is uncommon and so is this turtle. Its numbers are declining throughout its range due to habitat loss and collection for the pet trade. Turtle collectors are drawn to the species because of its small size. It rarely grows larger than four inches (10 cm), making it one of the smallest turtles in the world. The bog turtle is active only during the hottest parts of the day. On cool or cloudy days, it remains hidden in the mucky bottom of its habitat. It is easily disturbed from basking and dives into the water at the slightest noise.

Size: 3 to 4.5 inches (8 to 11.5 cm)

Range: Eastern North America

Habitat: Bogs, swamps, marshy meadows

Life Cycle: Egg-laying; three to six eggs laid June to July

MUSK TURTLE / *Sternotherus odoratus*

The common musk turtle is also known as a "stinkpot" or, in the southern United States, a "stinkin' Jim." Even its Latin name, *S. odoratus*, refers to the strong musk smell that the turtle is capable of emitting when handled or disturbed. The stench is produced by two pairs of small glands located just in front of the back legs. The males, which are much smaller than the females, have a spine-tipped tail that they use to manipulate and hold their mate's tail during copulation. The musk turtle doesn't dig a well-defined nest chamber; instead, the female simply scrapes away some debris and deposits her eggs under it. These turtles are known for their ability to climb, which allows them to bask on branches that overhang rivers.

Size: 3 to 5.5 inches (7 to 14 cm)

Range: Eastern North America

Habitat: Waterways with slow currents and soft bottoms

Life Cycle: Egg-laying; one to nine eggs per clutch, two to five clutches laid February to August

COMMON SNAPPING TURTLE / *Chelydra serpentina*

Size: 8 to 14 inches (20 to 36 cm)

Range: Central and eastern North America, south to Ecuador

Habitat: Freshwater habitats

Life Cycle: Egg-laying; eleven to eighty-three eggs laid May to September

With its big head, serrated carapace, and lumpy neck, the American snapping turtle looks prehistoric. And indeed it is: Snapping turtles have remained relatively unchanged for millions of years. Aquatic in nature, it often has algae growing on its shell, which serves as a camouflage. The species is usually observed just below the water's surface, only its eyes and nose protruding, although occasionally it is seen basking on land. Snappers cannot pull into their shell and are therefore vulnerable when they are out of the water. A snapper discovered on land should be treated with respect; this creature is capable of inflicting serious wounds.

EUROPEAN POND TURTLE / *Emys orbicularis*

This is the only living species in its genus and the only representative of the subfamily Emydidae in the Old World. It is easily recognized by the small yellow spots on the dark carapace and the top of the head. Males are distinguished from females by their red eyes; the eyes of females are yellow. Since this species occurs over such a large geographic range, its seasonal behaviors are quite varied. In the northern part of the range, it hibernates to avoid the cold winters, while in the southern part, it estivates— a state of torpor induced by heat— to avoid the hot summer. When not basking, the turtle can often be found in the vegetation along the banks of waterways, searching for insects, worms, salamanders, and frogs.

Size: 9 to 11 inches (22 to 28 cm)

Range: Europe, northwest Africa

Habitat: Slow-moving waterways with soft bottoms

Life Cycle: Egg-laying; three to sixteen eggs laid May to June

GIANT SNAKE-NECKED TURTLE / *Chelodina expansa*

Size: 12 to 19 inches (30 to 48 cm)

Range: Eastern Australia

Habitat: Permanent freshwater bodies

Life Cycle: Egg-laying; five to twenty-four eggs per clutch, three to four clutches laid March to May

The neck of these turtles is very long, hence the species' name. The snake-necks—or side-necks, as the whole group is called—are found only in the southern hemisphere and are the only non-marine turtles in Australia. The side-necks are unable to pull into their shell when threatened. Instead, they lay their head and neck along a groove between the carapace and the plastron. The giant snake-necked turtle is relatively calm when handled and does not produce the offensive odor that many others in this genus do. The incubation period for this species is very long. One nest was opened more than six hundred days after being built and the hatchlings were still alive.

SPOTTED POND TURTLE / *Geoclemys hamiltonii*

A rare species that can only be found in the drainage of the Indus and Ganges rivers, the spotted pond turtle lives in the reedy vegetation on riverbanks and feeds on invertebrates and small fishes. All turtles are facing a death sentence in southern Asia, where they are prized for their medicinal and health-giving properties; this includes the spotted pond turtle, a species that is now protected by the Convention on the International Trade of Endangered Species of Flora and Fauna (CITES). Turtles, although long-lived, have low reproductive rates and few species are unable to withstand the loss of breeding adults from the population.

Size: 11 to 15 inches (28 to 39 cm)

Range: Pakistan, India

Habitat: Large rivers, forest ponds

Life Cycle: Egg-laying; fifteen to thirty-five eggs per clutch, one to two clutches laid April to June

GHARIAL / *Gavialis gangeticus*

One of the largest and most aquatic of the living crocodilians, the gharial is also one of the most endangered. By 1970 fewer than five hundred remained across the creature's entire range, which once included Bhutan and Bangladesh. Fortunately, a conservation program was initiated focusing on hatching eggs and raising young in captivity before releasing them. Since then, the number of gharials has rebounded somewhat. The adult males grow a bulbous appendage at the end of their snout, which is very similar in shape to an Indian pot called a ghara, hence this species' common name.

Size: 236 to 276 inches (600 to 700 cm)

Range: India, Nepal, Pakistan

Habitat: Rivers

Life Cycle: Egg-laying; thirty to fifty eggs laid March to May

TUATARA / *Sphenodon punctatus*

This lizardlike reptile has roamed the planet since before the days of the dinosaurs. Often called a living fossil, it is one of two nearly identical surviving species of a family that originated during the Mesozoic period 220 million years ago. The animal has been in decline since humans first settled New Zealand, and it is now an endangered and fully protected species. Less than a hundred thousand tuataras survive, but the reptile is doing well on islands that are free of its worst enemy after man, the Polynesian rat, a predator that eats the tuatara's eggs. Tuataras can live up to a hundred years.

Size: Up to 26 inches (65 cm)

Range: Thirty small islands off mainland New Zealand

Habitat: Scrubby vegetation, forests

Life Cycle: Egg-laying; seven to ten eggs laid October to December every four years

Rain Forest

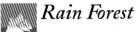

In tropical rain forests, rain falls every month of the year, reaching annual accumulations of at least eighty inches (200 cm). Some Latin American rain forests are drenched with up twenty times this amount. Days and nights are warm, averaging about eighty degrees Fahrenheit (27°C). Temperatures vary little from season to season. The heat, combined with the moist air, produces a dense canopy of tall trees so thick that little sunlight can reach the ground. The dominant vegetation consists of broad-leaved evergreen trees, such as mahogany, ironwood, and palm, and woody species, such as climbing lianas. Much of the secondary vegetation consists of plants such as bromeliads and orchids. The shade cast by these species allows relatively few low-growing plants to survive. However, a rich variety of vegetative life thrives in clearings and along the rivers that cut through the forest.

The largest tropical rain forests are located near the equator in Central and South America, central Africa, southeast Asia, and northern Australia. Tropical rain forests once covered more than four billion acres (1.6 billion ha), but they have been reduced during the last century by almost half. Rain forests also occur in temperate regions, such as the northwest coast of North America.

FINDING A NICHE

This life zone contains the greatest number of plant and animal species on Earth. With so much competition for resources, many amphibian and reptile species have adapted to a single rain-forest niche. For example, some snakes and lizards live their whole life in the uppermost reaches of the canopy, while others are found at lower levels or on the ground. A few species of tree frog live and reproduce in small pools of water that form in unfurling leaves. Other frog species, along with salamanders and turtles, live on the trunks of trees or in the leaf litter on the ground. Caecilians, meanwhile, rarely venture from their subterranean homes.

Lush and humid, rain forests contain more plant and animal species than any other life zone on the planet. While most rain forests are tropical, they are also found in temperate climates.

TLACONETE SALAMANDER / *Pseudoeurycea bellii*

Size: 9 to 13 inches (22 to 32 cm)

Range: Central Mexico

Habitat: Wet mountain forests

Life Cycle: Egg-laying; 25-50 eggs

This species is the largest member of the family Plethodontidae, a group of salamanders known as lungless salamanders. These animals breathe through their skin, which is why they are so long and skinny: Their shape increases the surface area of skin in relation to their volume. *P. bellii* is almost always found in moist areas since its skin must be wet to absorb oxygen. Females lay their eggs on land in moist depressions or under objects and remain with them until they hatch. The young emerge as fully metamorphosed miniatures of the adults. Unlike most salamanders, *P. bellii* is semi-arboreal and climbs with the use of its prehensile tail.

SOUTH AMERICAN BULLFROG / *Leptodactylus pentadactylus*

Size: 4 to 8 inches (10 to 20 cm)

Range: Central America to Brazil

Habitat: Semi-aquatic, usually close to water

Life Cycle: Egg-laying; eggs laid in floating bubble nest

The male South American bullfrog is highly territorial during mating season and will fight viciously with rivals, occasionally delivering fatal wounds with the bony spines in its feet. During egg laying and fertilization, the male creates a protective nest of bubbles by stirring together water, air, sperm, and egg jelly. The nest envelops the eggs and prevents desiccation, especially during dry periods when water levels may fluctuate. But the bubbles do not provide protection against such predators as parasitic flies, the hungry larvae of which will feed on this rich food source. Bullfrogs lay thousands of eggs so that a few might survive.

FALSE-EYED FROG / *Physalaemus nattereri*

Size: 1 to 1.3 inches (2.5 to 3.2 cm)

Range: Central and southeastern Brazil

Habitat: Rain forest

Life Cycle: Egg-laying

When the false-eyed frog is threatened, it puffs up its body and raises and angles its posterior toward the attacker, displaying two large "eyes." The sight of these large eyes is intended to make the attacker think that the animal it is attacking is bigger than is actually the case. The use of eyespots as a defense mechanism is employed by many types of insects, as well as some other frogs and a few birds. The tiny false-eyed frogs are extremely competitive during the breeding season. In order to increase their chance of attracting a mate, the males will increase the rate, loudness, and complexity of their calls.

FLEISCHMANN'S GLASS FROG / *Centrolenella fleischmannii*

Size: 0.6 to 0.8 inch (1.6 to 2.1 cm)

Range: Southern Mexico to northern South America

Habitat: Tropical forests close to streams

Life Cycle: Egg-laying; twenty-five to thirty eggs

Glass frogs are tiny, thin-limbed amphibians with large toe pads that help them move around in trees. They were given their name because the skin on their belly is thin and translucent, making their internal organs—including the beating heart—easily visible to the casual observer. These frogs are so delicate that reports exist of them being killed by large raindrops. The females lay their eggs on the underside of leaves above forest streams. After fertilizing them, the males stay close by to keep the eggs moist and guard them from predators. When they hatch, the tadpoles fall into the stream below to complete their metamorphosis.

GASTRIC BROODING FROG / *Rheobatrachus silus*

Last seen in the late 1980s and now assumed to be extinct, this frog was famous for its unique method of reproduction. After the eggs were laid and fertilized, the female would swallow them. The secretion of stomach juices was suspended and the stomach was used as an incubation chamber. Six to seven weeks later, fully metamorphosed froglets emerged from the mouth of the adult. Before this frog disappeared, scientists studied its digestion, hoping that the ability to suspend secretion of acids could be useful in the treatment of ulcers.

Size: 1.2 to 2 inches (3 to 5 cm)

Range: Southeast Queensland in Australia

Habitat: Rain-forest creeks and adjacent pools

Life Cycle: Egg-laying; eighteen to twenty-five eggs

GOLIATH FROG / *Conraua goliath*

Size: 8 to 12 inches (20 to 30 cm)

Range: Cameroon, equatorial Guinea in Africa

Habitat: Rain-forest streams

Life Cycle: Egg-laying

The goliath frog is the largest frog in the world. Individuals can weigh up to seven pounds (3.3 kg) and, with their legs extended, measure over 29.5 inches (75 cm) in length. Despite the frog's great size, its greenish brown coloration provides excellent camouflage among the wet, moss-covered rocks that line the fast-flowing rivers in its habitat. The range of the goliath frog is limited to a small strip of rain forest that measures less than 155 miles (250 km) by 62 miles (100 km). As a tadpole, it feeds on a single species of plant found near rapids and waterfalls. These factors make it highly vulnerable to population declines and eventual extinction.

HAIRY FROG / *Trichobatrachus robustus*

As its name implies, the male hairy frog has hairlike appendages on its flanks and thighs. The function of these filaments is unclear, but one theory holds that they serve as an external breathing apparatus for the male, which remains underwater with the eggs to guard them from predators until they hatch. Another theory proposes that the males release oxygen through these filaments into the water where the eggs are laid—on the underside of rocks in a chamber that the male has dug. Hairy frogs are a common food item among Cameroonians and are used in traditional medicine to increase fertility.

Size: 3 to 5 inches (7 to 12 cm)

Range: Eastern Nigeria to Zaire, Cameroon, equatorial Guinea

Habitat: Lowland rain forest, high or upland deciduous forests

Life Cycle: Egg-laying; eggs laid in dry season

HARLEQUIN FROG / *Atelopus flavescens*

The harlequin frog is actually a toad. The confusion stems at least in part from its smooth froglike skin. In addition to its bright pink belly, this species is renowned for the way males grasp females in amplexus (the mating grip) for up to four months before the breeding season even starts—a response to the fierce competition for mates. Female harlequin frogs have a call of their own, a characteristic shared by few other female frogs. Their eggs hatch within twenty-four hours, perhaps because they are often laid in fast-moving streams. The tadpoles have a large oral disc that allows them to latch onto rocks and feed on algae in this turbulent environment. When threatened, the frog exposes its bright underside to warn predators of its toxic skin secretions.

Size: 1.2 to 1.6 inches (3 to 4 cm)

Range: Northeastern South America

Habitat: Lowland rain forest

Life Cycle: Egg-laying

PARADOXICAL FROG / *Pseudis paradoxa*

For years, scientists observed enormous tadpoles eight to eleven inches (20 to 27 cm) long in lakes and ponds and reasoned that any frog with tadpoles that big must also be a giant. But repeated searches turned up no such amphibian. Eventually, it was realized that the abundant, almost totally aquatic frogs seen nearby—less than one third the size of the tadpoles—were actually the adult form of the species. Hence the paradox. The giant tadpoles have earned this frog another common name, the fish frog, alluding to a resemblance to a native fish. In fact, the tadpoles are so large that they are often sold alongside fish at local markets.

Size: 2 to 3 inches (5 to 7 cm)

Range: Northern South America

Habitat: Ponds, lakes, swamps in tropical lowlands

Life Cycle: Egg-laying

STRAWBERRY POISON-ARROW FROG / *Dendrobates pumilio*

Size: 0.8 to 1 inch (2 to 2.5 cm)

Range: Central America

Habitat: Lowland tropical forests

Life Cycle: Egg-laying; four to six eggs

Dendrobatids are famous for their brilliant warning colors and their highly toxic skin secretions. In a form of behavior rare among amphibians, the strawberry poison-arrow frog provides food for its young. After hatching, the tadpoles wriggle up and are secured to the mother's back with a sticky skin secretion. They are then carried to a pool of water at the base of a bromeliad leaf. There, the tadpoles complete development, feeding on infertile eggs that the female regularly deposits for each offspring. This high degree of parental care is an adaptation to the frog's small size and its production of relatively few eggs.

WALLACE'S FLYING FROG / *Rhacophorus nigropalmatus*

Size: 3 to 4 inches (8 to 10 cm)

Range: Southeast Asia

Habitat: Primary and secondary tropical rain forest and forest edges

Life Cycle: Egg-laying

Alfred Russel Wallace, after whom this frog is named, was the first to report on the amphibian's aerial abilities. Extending its heavily webbed feet and contorting its body shape to concave, the Wallace's flying frog is able to create enough air resistance when it jumps to enable it to land several yards from its point of departure, with some degree of maneuverability. Called parachuting or gliding by some, the behavior also became known as "plopping" in herpetological literature after some students used the term jokingly in reference to a dead frog used as a control to study the time of descent of live frogs. A Malaysian relative has accomplished "flights" of more than 33 feet (10 m).

BRAZILIAN HORNED TOAD / *Ceratophrys cornuta*

Size: 6 to 8 inches (16 to 20 cm)

Range: Brazil, northeast South America

Habitat: Forest floor

Life Cycle: Egg-laying

This peculiar-looking toad gets its name from the pointy, hornlike pieces of skin above its eyes. It is believed that the protuberances, along with the toad's dark brown and tan mottling, help to camouflage it. Almost as wide as it is long, the horned toad is nearly circular. Its huge head and mouth account for almost 50 percent of its body. Other toads form the bulk of this carnivorous toad's diet. Its camouflage helps it to hide and ambush its prey. The toad lures prey by gently wiggling its toes. When a victim comes close enough, the toad lunges forward open-mouthed and stuffs dinner into its mouth by hand.

GOLDEN TOAD / *Bufo periglenes*

The particularly rapid decline and apparent extinction of the golden toad helped focus attention on the plight of amphibians around the world. The golden toad is—or was—native to Monte Verde, where it would hide out among the roots of trees and in underground cavities for most of the year. Up until the early 1980s, hundreds of them would suddenly appear after heavy rains and breed in accumulated ponds of water. By the mid-1980s, however, the population was severely depleted and in 1989 only one adult was seen. None has been found since.

Size: 2.2 to 2.8 inches (5.5 to 7 cm)

Range: Monte Verde Cloud Forest Reserve, Costa Rica

Habitat: Cloud forests

Life Cycle: Egg-laying; eggs laid in April

SURINAM TOAD / *Pipa pipa*

Size: 4 to 8 inches (10 to 20 cm)

Range: South America, excluding southern regions

Habitat: Aquatic environments

Life Cycle: Egg-laying; forty to sixty eggs

Despite its staring, beady eyes, this unusually flattened animal is well camouflaged. It inhabits muddy waterways, relying on its long sensitive fingers to feel around in the mud at night for its favorite food, invertebrates. Since this toad feeds while underwater, it stuffs food into its mouth with its fingers, rather than catching food with its tongue, as most toads do. In a reproductive display that can only be described as acrobatic, the male grips the female and they do somersaults while mating. At each turn, the female lets out eggs and the male fertilizes them, then pushes them into the spongy back of the female. The skin on the female's back then grows around the eggs, protecting them as they develop into toadlets.

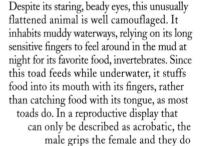

WHITE'S TREE FROG / *Litoria caerulea*

Sometimes referred to as the "dumpy frog" because it has large folds of skin that look like fat, the White's tree frog is often heard calling from high in the trees. During dry spells, it is commonly encountered around human habitations searching for water and food. Its appealing face and charming disposition (it can be taught to eat food off a human finger) have created a demand for the species as a pet. It is now protected in most of Australia. Extracts from the skin have been used for many medicinal uses, including fighting a staphylococcus bacterium that can cause abscesses, helping to lower human blood pressure, and treating the cold-sore herpes virus.

Size: 2 to 4 inches (6 to 11 cm)

Range: Northern and eastern Australia to southern New Guinea

Habitat: Close to streams or in swamps

Life Cycle: Egg-laying; two hundred to two thousand eggs laid November to February

BLUE-RINGED CAECILIAN / *Siphonops annulatus*

Size: 12 to 17 inches (30 to 43 cm)

Range: Central and eastern South America

Habitat: Tropical forests

Life Cycle: Egg-laying

Most species of caecilians are shades of gray, brown, or black, but the blue-ringed caecilian is more brightly colored. Caecilians are a separate order of amphibians and have evolved to be almost totally subterranean, with a rigid skull to help them push through the soil, reduced eyes that are often below the skin, and countersunk jaws that help prevent soil from getting in their mouth. Little is known about these animals because they live underground, rarely coming to the surface, and are very difficult to find. The blue-ringed caecilian has very sensitive tentacles beneath its rudimentary eyes; the tentacles are used to aid them in detecting prey.

STICKY CAECILIAN / *Ichthyophus glutinosus*

Size: 10 to 16 inches (25 to 40 cm)

Range: Malayan archipelago

Habitat: Rain forest

Life Cycle: Egg-laying; twenty to thirty eggs

With its skin covered in a sticky residue, the sticky caecilian is aptly named. This wormlike creature spends most of its time underground in damp forests, coming to the surface only during or shortly after heavy rains. Females dig small egg chambers close to water and coil around the eggs that they lay there to provide them with moisture and protection. When the eggs hatch, the finned larvae quickly move to water, living there until they are about four inches (10 cm) long. They then leave the water and dig into the bank, where they undergo many physical changes, including loss of a kind of tail fin. They cannot return to the water after this or they will drown.

RUBBER EEL / *Typhlonectes natans*

Despite its name, the rubber eel is actually a caecilian, an obscure group of amphibians with a legless, cylindrical body shape adapted to a burrowing lifestyle. Most of these wormlike creatures are terrestrial, but the rubber eel and the seventeen other species found in the family Typhlonectidae are aquatic. They all have a well-developed mouth for catching and eating their prey and a body that is slightly flattened toward the rear to improve their ability to swim. Although similar in appearance to an eel, they are easily distinguished because they do not have fins or gills.

Size: 14 to 29 inches (35 to 50 cm)

Range: Northwestern Columbia

Habitat: Streams with rocky bottoms

Life Cycle: Live-bearing

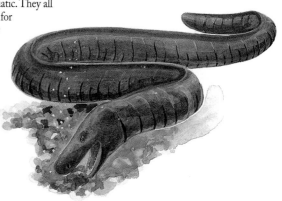

GREEN BASILISK / *Basiliscus plumifrons*

The green basilisk is also known as the Jesus Christ lizard because it is capable of walking—actually running—on water, the result of rear feet with modified scales that increase the foot's surface area *(page 51)*. It is only capable of running over smooth water; if it breaks the surface tension, the lizard will sink. This mode of travel is most often employed as an escape mechanism from predators. The green basilisk is one of the few lizards that utilize bipedal locomotion instead of walking on all fours. The word basilisk refers to an ancient Greek mythological part-lizard monster with brilliant yellow eyes that could turn people to stone simply by looking at them.

Size: 20 to 27.5 inches (50 to 70 cm)

Range: Guatemala to Costa Rica

Habitat: Rain forest close to water

Life Cycle: Egg-laying; five to twenty eggs

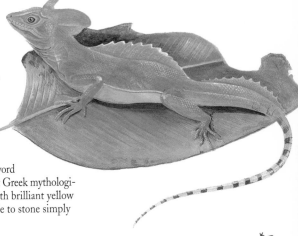

JACKSON'S CHAMELEON / *Chamaeleo jacksonii*

Size: 6 to 10 inches (15 to 25 cm)

Range: Eastern Africa, introduced in Hawaii

Habitat: Rain forest

Life Cycle: Live-bearing; five to forty young

The Jackson's chameleon is easily distinguished from other chameleons by the three large horns on its head. Although it is a rainforest species, the chameleon is also adaptable and has learned to live in the more open environments created by forestry and agriculture. In fact, Jackson's chameleons are often found in higher densities in these disturbed areas because of the increase in food items such as crop pests. Most chameleons are egg layers, but this species has adapted to life at high, cool elevations by retaining its eggs and bearing live young. It has been introduced to Hawaii, where it is now common.

FLYING DRAGON / *Draco volans*

Size: 7 to 8 inches (17 to 21 cm)

Range: Southeastern Asia, associated islands

Habitat: Tropical forests

Life Cycle: Egg-laying

A slender arboreal lizard, the flying dragon is well camouflaged. Looking a lot like the tree branches among which it spends most of its time, this lizard is quite unimpressive until it spreads its orange and black wings. There are at least twenty species of flying dragons, all with comparably brilliant wing coloration—sometimes said to rival that of a butterfly.

The wings are actually flaps of skin stretched over outward-projecting elongated ribs, which can be opened to allow the lizard to glide long distances. Scientists believe that this anatomical feature probably evolved for mating or territorial display, with a flying role developing later.

COMMON MADAGASCAR DAY GECKO / *Phelsuma madagascariensis*

Most geckos are nocturnal, but the common Madagascar day gecko is active during the daytime. Its toes are slightly enlarged and have numerous small ridges that help it grip and climb trees. *P. madagascariensis* has an unusual defense strategy. Rather than flee or face a predator, the lizard just lets go and falls from its arboreal perch, using its tail as a rudder and for balance. Like a cat, it always lands on its feet. In its homeland, the common Madagascar day gecko has adapted well to human habitation and can often be seen chasing insects across walls and roofs. Its brilliant coloration has helped make it a popular pet.

Size: 7 to 9.4 inches (18 to 24 cm)

Range: Madagascar

Habitat: Forest edges

Life Cycle: Egg-laying; two eggs per clutch, multiple clutches laid November to April

NEW CALEDONIAN CRESTED GECKO / *Rhacodactylus ciliatus*

Size: 7 to 8 inches (17 to 21 cm)

Range: New Caledonia, Isle of Pines off east coast of Australia

Habitat: Clearings in primary forests with moderate vegetation and layer of leaf litter

Life Cycle: Egg-laying; one to two eggs laid throughout year

This nocturnal and semi-arboreal gecko gets its common name from an eyelashlike crest that starts above the eye and continues laterally to the shoulder. The gecko's shovel-like head and snout are used to burrow under leaf litter, where the animal hides during the day. The species was thought to have become extinct until small populations were found in the early 1990s. Smuggling for the pet trade after its rediscovery threatened this beautiful lizard, but captive breeding has effectively stopped that trend by making wild-caught specimens more expensive than their captive-bred counterparts.

THAI BOW-FINGERED GECKO / *Cyrtodactylus peguensis*

Size: 4 to 5 inches (10 to 13 cm)

Range: Thailand, Burma

Habitat: Forested areas along banks of rivers and streams

Life Cycle: Egg-laying; two eggs

While it is difficult to distinguish this species from other bow-fingered geckos, identifying markings include darker flecking and a stripe that runs from behind the eye to the ear opening. Many geckos have ridged, suction-cuplike discs on their feet, but bow-fingered geckos have bent, or bowed, toes with claws. This does not hinder them from being fast and agile climbers, however. Bow-fingered geckos have become popular items in the exotic-pet trade. With their need for a high-humidity environment, many individuals caught in the wild have perished during shipping. It is hoped that improvements in captive-breeding programs will shrink the market for wild-caught individuals.

TOKAY GECKO / *Gecko gecko*

The tokay gecko has adapted well to human-inhabited areas, where it eats almost anything that it can shove into its mouth. This quality has endeared it to many people because it keeps pest species such as cockroaches under control. But not all traits of the tokay gecko earn approval. It is highly aggressive and will often hiss and open its mouth wide. If bothered further, it will attack and lock onto its foe with teeth that won't let go. The lizard is named for the loud croaking "tokay, tokay" sound it makes. The species has been used in medicines throughout Asia and more recently has become popular in the pet trade.

Size: 8 to 12 inches (20 to 30 cm)

Range: Southeast Asia

Habitat: Rain forest, adapted to life in cities

Life Cycle: Egg-laying; eggs laid in pairs throughout year

GREEN IGUANA / *Iguana iguana*

Also called the common iguana, this species is the most widely distributed and abundant of all iguanas. It has a crest of teethlike scales running along its back and tail; this crest is more pronounced in the males. The green iguana is a good climber and swimmer, spending much of its time basking, foraging, and sleeping in trees, and will drop into the water below if disturbed. The females will nest communally—up to two hundred in one site—usually constructing shallow burrows in sandy soils. Because its eggs and the meat are a delicacy in many Central and South American regions, the green iguana is commonly called *gallino de palo*, or "chicken of the tree."

Size: 51 to 71 inches (130 to 180 cm)

Range: Mexico to southern Brazil and Paraguay, some Caribbean islands

Habitat: Humid forests with dense canopies, often in trees overhanging water

Life Cycle: Egg-laying; thirty to seventy eggs laid in dry season

CROCODILE MONITOR / *Varanus salvadorii*

Like other monitors, the crocodile monitor has the unusual habit of standing on its hindlegs to look around. Some native people believe that it uses the extra height to watch for crocodiles; if it spots one, it will give a warning call. There are many folktales relating to these lizards. It is erroneously said, for example, that monitors are venomous. This belief probably arose from the fact that they are capable of delivering a nasty bite, some of those bites having led to fatal infections, the result of the heavy concentration of bacteria in the monitor's mouth rather than venom.

Size: 91 to 118 inches (230 to 300 cm)

Range: New Guinea

Habitat: Tropical forests

Life Cycle: Egg-laying

FIRE SKINK / *Riopa fernandii*

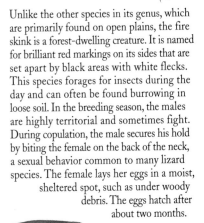

Size: 9 to 14 inches (23 to 35 cm)

Range: West Africa

Habitat: Forested areas

Life Cycle: Egg-laying; five to nine eggs

Unlike the other species in its genus, which are primarily found on open plains, the fire skink is a forest-dwelling creature. It is named for brilliant red markings on its sides that are set apart by black areas with white flecks. This species forages for insects during the day and can often be found burrowing in loose soil. In the breeding season, the males are highly territorial and sometimes fight. During copulation, the male secures his hold by biting the female on the back of the neck, a sexual behavior common to many lizard species. The female lays her eggs in a moist, sheltered spot, such as under woody debris. The eggs hatch after about two months.

COMMON TEGU / *Tupinambis teguixin*

Size: 28 to 47 inches (70 to 120 cm)

Range: Eastern South America

Habitat: Tropical woodlands and forests

Life Cycle: Egg-laying

The scientific name for this species comes partly from a now-vanished Brazilian tribe called the Tupinamba. In the Tupi language, *tegu* meant lizard, while *ixia* is from the Greek for plant, a reference to the leaves and fruits that the tegu eats in its nightly foraging. Its diet also includes small mammals, birds, eggs, amphibians, and worms. The females lay their eggs in termite mounds that they rip open. After the termites repair the damage, the mounds provide the eggs with a safe, warm, moist environment in which to develop.

GREEN ANACONDA / *Eunectes murinus*

Although there are stories—all almost certainly false—of sixty-foot (18-m) -long anacondas, members of this species seldom exceed 30 feet (9.5 m) in length. Nonetheless, the green anaconda is one of the largest snakes in the world. It is also among the heaviest: Some specimens have a girth of more than thirty-nine inches (100 cm). This diurnal giant usually lies partially submerged in water, where its dappled coloration and patterning serve as camouflage. It patiently waits for birds, caimans, large rodents, and other mammals to venture near the water, seizing them in its mouth and killing them by constriction.

Size: 276 to 393 inches (700 to 1,000 cm)

Range: South America, except Argentina, Chile, Uruguay

Habitat: Aquatic environments in tropical forests and savanna

Life Cycle: Live-bearing; four to forty young born January to August depending on geographic location

EMERALD TREE BOA / *Corallus caninus*

With its vivid green color, the emerald tree boa is well camouflaged for life high in the forest canopy. It is a nocturnal species that hunts small mammals, birds, and occasionally lizards and spends its days in a characteristic coil draped over a branch. The white markings along its back help in concealing it during the day by breaking up its outline. This boa has two features that help it capture food: large, strong teeth; and a prehensile tail that grips onto a branch as the snake strikes out to capture prey passing close by. In one of the most striking examples of convergent evolution, this boa has evolved the same characteristics of size, color, shape, and behavior as New Guinea's green tree python (*Morelia viridis*).

Size: 47 to 71 inches (120 to 180 cm)

Range: Northern and central South America

Habitat: Lowland tropical rain forest

Life Cycle: Live-bearing; two to fifteen young

PACIFIC GROUND BOA / *Candoia carinata*

Size: 20 to 39 inches (50 to 100 cm)

Range: Celebes, Papua–New Guinea, Solomon Island, Tokelaue Island

Habitat: Forested regions

Life Cycle: Live-bearing; five to fifteen young born September to January

The one constant with this species is its sharply angled snout. Coloration and pattern, on the other hand, are highly variable. This snake can be any shade of cream, tan, yellow, orange, red, beige, gray, or black, overlaid on striped, banded, blotchy, or solid patterning. And depending on the temperature, time of day, and humidity, it can change color slightly. Like all boas, this species ambushes and constricts its prey, mainly small rodents and lizards. It is quite similar to two other species that belong to the same genus, *Candoia*. One species, *C. bibronii*, is longer and thinner and primarily arboreal. *C. aspersa* is terrestrial and much shorter and thicker. *C. carinata*, meanwhile, is both arboreal and terrestrial.

BUSHMASTER / *Lachesis muta*

The bushmaster—subject of many myths and folktales— is the longest venomous snake in Latin America and the largest of all the pit vipers. The Latin name means "silent fate" and refers to the highly toxic bite, which can cause death within a few hours. When agitated, the snake will vibrate its hard, pointed tail, producing a high-pitched buzz, and will sometimes strike without warning. With its contrasting diamond-blotched pattern and its coarse scales, the bushmaster is sometimes referred to as *mapapire ananas*, or pineapple snake.

Size: 87 to 148 inches (220 to 375 cm)

Range: Nicaragua to northern South America, Trinidad

Habitat: Tropical upland rain forest

Life Cycle: Egg-laying; ten to twelve eggs

CORAL PIPESNAKE / *Anilius scytale*

The only New World member of the family Aniliidae, the coral pipesnake is sometimes called the two-headed snake because of its habit of hiding in a burrow when threatened and leaving only its tail—which looks little different from its head—poking out of the ground. The blunt head is one of several features that adapt the snake to its burrowing lifestyle. It also has eyes that are covered by transparent scales to keep dirt out. The coral pipesnake is occasionally referred to as a false coral snake because of a color and patterning similar to its venomous cousin—a likeness that may provide the coral pipesnake with some protection from predators.

Size: 20 to 35 inches (50 to 90 cm)

Range: Northern South America

Habitat: Rain forest and open woodlands

Life Cycle: Live-bearing; nine to sixteen young born January to February

RETICULATED PYTHON / *Python reticulatus*

Size: 197 to 360 inches (500 to 900 cm)

Range: Southeastern Asia, nearby islands

Habitat: Tropical forests, usually close to water

Life Cycle: Egg-laying; forty-five to eighty eggs

The reticulated python is one of the world's largest snakes. There are reliable reports of "retics"—as herpetologists sometimes call them—more than thirty feet (9 m) long. Despite its size, the snake is extremely diffi- cult to observe in its natural environment because of its camouflage: elaborate pattern- ing that matches well with the thick vegeta- tion or leaf layer where it lies motionless during the day. In its nightly hunting, the snake eats birds and mid-sized mammals, such as deer and pigs. It has on occasion also feasted on small children. Reticulated pythons are often exploited for leather because of their large size.

BRAHMINY BLIND SNAKE / *Rhamphotyphlops bramina*

Size: 4 to 7 inches (11 to 17 cm)

Range: Southeast Asia, introduced to South Africa, Australia, southeastern North America, Hawaii, Mexico

Habitat: Many habitats throughout tropical and subtropical regions

Life Cycle: Egg-laying; two to six eggs

This slender burrower has successfully colo- nized most tropical and subtropical regions of the world because it can reproduce without a mate. Known as parthenogenetic repro- duction, this adaptation enables a single individual to populate an area, a capability the blind snake shares with certain species of invertebrates, fish, salamanders, and lizards. The small size and burrow- ing habits of the blind snake have enabled it to move around the world in potted plants, which accounts for its other common name, the flower-pot snake.

FLYING SNAKE / *Chrysopelea ornata*

Size: 28 to 47 inches (70 to 120 cm)

Range: Southeastern Asia

Habitat: Rain forest

Life Cycle: Egg-laying; six to twelve eggs laid February to March

A flying snake? That's a bit of an exaggeration, but *C. ornata* is capable of something approaching gliding to move from tree to tree. The snake coils its body and then launches itself from a branch, flattening out its body and making its belly scales concave to create more air resistance. This slows its descent and decreases the force of impact when the snake lands on another branch. A swift, agile climber, the flying snake is often found at the top of trees, where it hunts for geckos and other lizards, as well as frogs and small birds.

LONG-NOSED VINE SNAKE / *Ahaetulla nasuta*

Size: 39 to 79 inches (100 to 200 cm)

Range: Sri Lanka and India to Thailand

Habitat: Tropical rain forest

Life Cycle: Live-bearing; young born throughout year

With its earthy colors, this slender vinelike snake blends in superbly with its arboreal environment. In fact, its body is so well adapted to a tree-dwelling lifestyle that it has difficulty moving on the ground and almost never leaves the forest canopy. It hunts arboreal lizards utilizing a sit-and-wait strategy, remaining motionless until its victim comes within range. Long-nosed vine snakes have keen binocular vision—rare in snakes—which enables them to judge distance when moving from branch to branch. They rely more heavily on their excellent vision than other species of snakes, which depend mainly on their keen sense of smell.

MAINLAND TIGER SNAKE / *Notechis scutatus*

One of the deadliest snakes in the world, the mainland tiger snake is responsible for most of the snakebite fatalities in Australia. When directly threatened or attacked, the snake rises up and flattens its neck and head to form a hood, much as the cobra does, before striking. Like most snakes, however, it prefers to slither away and hide rather than face down a potential predator. Because of the fear it inspires, it has been killed in great numbers over the years. This, along with a reduction in its habitats, has resulted in population declines. Public awareness campaigns have begun to reverse the trend.

Size: 37 to 55 inches (95 to 140 cm)
Range: Southeastern Australia
Habitat: Variable, from rain forest to grasslands
Life Cycle: Live-bearing; 17 to 109 young

RED-TAILED RAT SNAKE / *Gonyosoma oxycephala*

Size: 59 to 90.5 inches (150 to 230 cm)
Range: Southeastern Asia, Indonesian islands
Habitat: Rain forest and mangrove swamps
Life Cycle: Egg-laying; five to twelve eggs

While its name suggests otherwise, this snake's tail is typically a shade of brown, gray, or orange. The rest of the body is usually green, although in some members of the species it is brown, reddish brown, or gray. In an adaptation common to many tree-dwelling species, the red-tailed snake has a laterally-compressed body type that can support its weight as it stretches out to climb from branch to branch. A diurnal hunter, it locates its prey by picking up chemical signals in the air with flicks of its bright blue tongue. The snake's diet includes lizards, birds, bats, and other small mammals. Although non-venomous, it is aggressive and will readily bite to defend itself.

143

MATAMATA / *Chelus fimbriatus*

The only species in its genus, the matamata is a master of camouflage. Its flattened, ridged shell looks like a piece of bark covered with algae, while its flat-shaped head and neck have loose flaps of skin that look like dead leaves. These flaps of skin sway in the current like small pieces of aquatic vegetation and attract small animals, usually fish. Once the prey is within range, the turtle opens it mouth and expands its throat, sucking in its victim. This so-called gape-and-suck feeding method is also employed by other turtles. The matamata prefers shallow water so it can walk slowly along the bottom with only its nose out to breathe.

Size: 14 to 18 inches (35 to 45 cm)

Range: North-central South America

Habitat: Blackwater streams and stagnant pools

Life Cycle: Egg-laying; twelve to twenty-eight eggs laid October to December

PIG-NOSE TURTLE / *Carettochelys insculpta*

Size: 16 to 22 inches (40 to 55 cm)

Range: Southern New Guinea to northern Australia

Habitat: Rivers, streams, lakes, lagoons

Life Cycle: Egg-laying; fifteen eggs laid September to November

Also called the New Guinea river turtle, the pig-nose was once thought to be one of the rarest turtles in the world. Although it is uncommon, its scarcity stemmed from the fact that natives hired to assist researchers in collecting specimens often helped themselves to the pig-nose, which they considered a local delicacy. The forelimbs of the pig-nose are like the flippers of sea turtles—an unusual adaptation for a freshwater turtle. Like sea turtles, this species "flies" through the water, using its hindlimbs as rudders. The omnivorous pig-nose eats many invertebrates as well as leaves, roots, and seeds of aquatic plants.

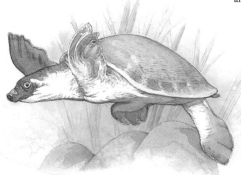

SOUTH AMERICAN RIVER TURTLE / *Podocnemis expansa*

This olive-brown to dark gray species is the largest in the genus *Podocnemis*. Most river turtles are omnivorous, but the South American variety is almost entirely herbivorous, feeding on vegetation and the fruits of aquatic plants, as well as any other fruits that might drop into rivers from overhanging trees. Once extremely abundant, South American river turtles are now threatened because of exploitation by Indians, who sometimes keep the animals alive in pens for months as a source of fresh meat. The turtles nest in large congregations in bare, sandy areas. Unfortunately, this makes them extremely vulnerable to egg collectors, who harvest the eggs to extract a high-grade oil that is used for burning in lanterns, lubricating machinery, and frying food.

Size: 28 to 35 inches (70 to 90 cm)

Range: North-central South America

Habitat: Large rivers and tributaries, adjacent lagoons and ponds

Life Cycle: Egg-laying; 63 to 136 eggs laid September to March, depending on geographic location

COMMON CAIMAN / *Caiman crocodilus*

Size: 59 to 98 inches (150 to 250 cm)

Range: Southern Mexico through northern South America to Brazil

Habitat: Small lakes and slow-moving streams with muddy bottoms

Life Cycle: Egg-laying; fourteen to forty eggs laid August to November

The common caiman is often called the spectacled caiman because of a bony ridge in front of its eyes that looks like the nose bow from a pair of spectacles. A close relative, called the smooth-fronted caiman, lacks this bony ridge. Because its skin has bony deposits in it, the caiman is one of the few species of crocodilians that was not threatened during the early part of this century. But as the more valuable species declined, hunters turned to caimans and they have been since been heavily exploited—not just adults for their skin, but also the young as stuffed novelty items.

Grasslands & Savanna

In certain areas with little rainfall or where the soil is too shallow for trees, grasses become the dominant vegetation, their shallow, spreading root systems efficiently seeking out whatever nutrients and water are available. Savanna is distinguished from grasslands by the presence of scattered trees or shrubs. Grasslands and savanna are found on every continent and include the steppes of Europe and Asia, the North American prairies, the pampas of South America, the Australian outback, and the African Savanna. These areas are often transition zones between woodlands and desert. Both reptiles and moisture-dependent amphibians can be found here—species that are adapted to both ingest or absorb sufficient quantities of moisture and retain it in the body.

Reptiles have thicker, less permeable skin, which makes them more tolerant than amphibians of drier conditions. Although evaporative water loss still occurs across the skin, water intake from drinking, eating, and absorption can offset this loss. Similar to birds, liquid waste is mostly uric acid.

With their moist skin, amphibians are very susceptible to water loss through evaporation—though some species can survive a loss of up to 50 percent of their body weight from dehydration. To keep moist, many amphibians dig burrows or use burrows dug by other animals. In Arizona, the spadefoot toad can burrow to depths of thirty-five inches (90 cm) and absorb moisture from soil holding as little as 3 percent water. To retard water loss during periods of dormancy or drought, some burrowing species create a cocoon from multiple layers of shed skin.

Another way amphibians deal with the drying effects of the elements is by tucking their limbs in close to the body so they are not exposed. Some salamanders curl their body and tail into tight coils, while anurans are sometimes found living in closely-packed clusters to keep moist. Many amphibians can flatten themselves on the ground to absorb more moisture. They also can minimize moisture loss by remaining inactive during the day. With their burrowing and nocturnal habits, grassland and savanna amphibians are rarely seen by humans.

Grasslands and savanna are dry areas that are often located between woodlands and desert. Amphibians in this biome have developed a variety of ways for seeking out and retaining moisture.

TIGER SALAMANDER / *Ambystoma tigrinum*

Not only is this one of the largest salamanders in North America, it is the most widely distributed. The tiger salamander can be found in almost any type of habitat, from forest to grassland to semi-desert. All it needs to thrive is a non-moving body of water in which to deposit its eggs. Due to its relatively large size, it is also capable of laying many eggs, as many as one thousand to two thousand in one evening. There are eight subspecies of the tiger salamander, diffusing in color pattern, morphology and geographic distribution.

Size: 7 to 13 inches (18 to 33 cm)

Range: Scattered across North America

Habitat: Found in many habitats, predominantly grasslands

Life Cycle: Egg-laying; 20 to 120 eggs per clutch, four to ten clutches laid throughout year

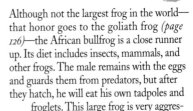

AFRICAN BULLFROG / *Pyxicephalus adspersus*

Size: 5 to 9 inches (12 to 24 cm)

Range: Sub-Sahara Africa

Habitat: Semi-desert grasslands and savanna

Life Cycle: Egg-laying; three thousand to four thousand eggs

Although not the largest frog in the world—that honor goes to the goliath frog *(page 126)*—the African bullfrog is a close runner up. Its diet includes insects, mammals, and other frogs. The male remains with the eggs and guards them from predators, but after they hatch, he will eat his own tadpoles and froglets. This large frog is very aggressive and the three small toothlike projections in the lower jaw are capable of inflicting a bite that won't soon be forgotten. It estivates underground for ten months of the year. The outer layers of skin are shed and, when combined with mucous secretions, harden into a cocoon that prevents water loss until the rains come.

ANSWERING FROG / *Microhyla berdmorei*

This frog is actually a toad that belongs to the narrow-mouthed family Microhylidae. By far the prettiest toad in its family, with a pinkish background color and dark brown marbling and light spotting and striping, this is an extremely difficult species to find because of its small size and tendency to hide in leaf litter. When one member of the species broadcasts its call (a buzzing sound), a neighboring one will buzz back, hence the name. At times when the answering frog is not calling, it feeds on ants and termites.

Size: 0.6 to 0.8 inch (1.5 to 2 cm)
Range: Southeast Asia
Habitat: Leaf litter in grasslands
Life Cycle: Egg-laying

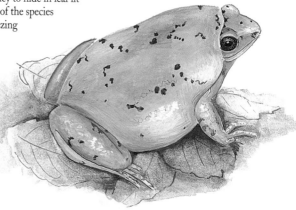

CHORUS FROG / *Pseudacris triseriata*

Size: 0.8 to 1.6 inches (2 to 4 cm)
Range: Central and southeastern North America
Habitat: Grasslands, woodlands, forests, swamps, agricultural lands, suburbs
Life Cycle: Egg-laying

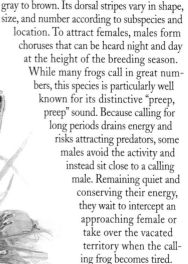

This small frog varies in color from greenish gray to brown. Its dorsal stripes vary in shape, size, and number according to subspecies and location. To attract females, males form choruses that can be heard night and day at the height of the breeding season. While many frogs call in great numbers, this species is particularly well known for its distinctive "preep, preep" sound. Because calling for long periods drains energy and risks attracting predators, some males avoid the activity and instead sit close to a calling male. Remaining quiet and conserving their energy, they wait to intercept an approaching female or take over the vacated territory when the calling frog becomes tired.

MOTTLED BURROWING FROG / *Hemisus marmoratum*

Size: 1 to 1.6 inches (2.5 to 4 cm)

Range: Southeastern Africa

Habitat: Grasslands

Life Cycle: Egg-laying

While most frogs and toads that burrow use their hind feet, the mottled burrowing frog tunnels in head-first, using its snout to push into the soft soil. Scientists once believed that the female frog laid her eggs in a cavity under a bank at the edge of a pool and then dug a tunnel down from the nest to the water as a passageway for the tadpoles. The truth isn't much different. The female lays her eggs in dry seasonal pools or at the edge of wet ones and sits on them, keeping them moist and protecting them from ants. Once the eggs hatch, the female plows a slide to the water and the tadpoles wiggle along it with her assistance.

PAINTED REED FROG / *Hyperolius marmoratus*

Size: 1 to 1.2 inches (2.5 to 3 cm)

Range: Central and southern Africa

Habitat: Vegetation adjacent to water in grasslands

Life Cycle: Egg-laying; four to twelve eggs per clutch, thirty to fifty clutches laid throughout year

Trying to identify this frog by color and pattern can prove difficult, since there are many colors of reed frog, and patterns range from striped to streaked and dotted to marbled. Not only that, but when exposed to bright light, the frog's colors fade or change. Scientists used to think that many of these different patterns and colors indicated different species. Today it is understood that there are just a few similar species and a larger number of subspecies. At night around ponds in its habitat, the reed frog pierces the silence with its loud, rapid, high-pitched call. It is named for the way it hangs from reeds and rushes with the suckerlike discs on its toes.

RAIN FROG / *Breviceps adspersus*

This species belongs to the genus *Breviceps*, which means "short head," an accurate description of this small-headed frog. It is known by locals as the rain frog because it starts calling in huge numbers in the rain, as many frogs do. As a result of living in a relatively dry habitat, this frog has developed small, spadelike tubercles on its hind feet that it uses for digging burrows into damp places to live. The female lays a relatively small number of larger-than-average eggs and hides them in underground nests or under rocks. Metamorphosis occurs inside the egg. When threatened, this frog inflates its body to startle and confuse predators.

Size: 2 to 2.4 inches (5 to 6 cm)
Range: Southern Africa
Habitat: Grasslands, shrubby areas
Life Cycle: Egg-laying

RED BANDED RUBBER FROG / *Phrynomerus bifasciatus*

Size: 1.6 to 2.8 inches (4 to 7 cm)
Range: Eastern, central, and southern Africa
Habitat: Open grasslands, shrubby areas
Life Cycle: Egg-laying; one thousand to fifteen hundred eggs

Named for its bright red stripes and rubbery skin, this frog secretes toxins that are fatal to other frogs and can cause rashes on human skin. Its diet of ants and termites is thought to be the source of this caustic substance, as it is for poison-arrow frogs. The frog's bright stripes may be an example of warning coloration, but because this species is nocturnal, potential predators would have to be capable of seeing these colors in the dark— something that has not been established. To confuse the issue further, when exposed to sunlight, the frog loses its bright stripes and turns pale gray and black. Because the frog walks rather than hops, it is known to some as the walking frog.

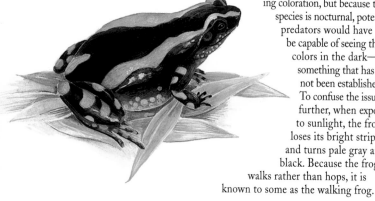

PLAINS SPADEFOOT / *Scaphiopus bombifrons*

This grassland toad estivates underground for long periods of time, relying on its strong limbs and spadelike feet to burrow backward into the loose soil. It comes out on rainy nights and during seasonal wet periods to forage and reproduce in temporary pools of water. The males gather at the breeding sites and their resonating ducklike call can be heard from far away, attracting the females to the water source. The females lay a large number of eggs, which develop into omnivorous and sometimes cannibalistic tadpoles within forty-eight hours. Metamorphosis is also quick, since the young must complete their development before the temporary pools dry up.

Size: 1.4 to 2 inches (3.5 to 5 cm)

Range: Central North America

Habitat: Dry grassland regions with loose soil

Life Cycle: Egg-laying; ten to two hundred eggs laid May to August

MONTANE SQUEAKER / *Arthroleptis adolfifriderici*

This frog earns its name from its high-pitched vocalizations, broadcast day and night in the rainy season. During the breeding season, the male montane squeaker will call "weep, weep, weepee, weep" to attract females. The call of a male frog is thought to have certain qualities that help a female to determine a good mate. For example, a very loud call may indicate a strong male. The healthy genes of the father are then passed on to the young.

Size: 1.2 to 1.8 inches (3 to 4.5 cm)

Range: Central southern Africa

Habitat: Upland grasslands and forests

Life Cycle: Egg-laying

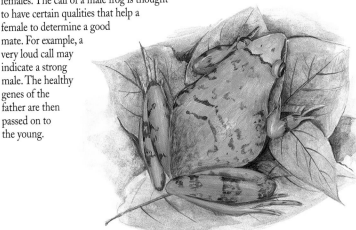

151

COMMON AGAMA / *Agama agama*

Like the chameleon, the common agama is capable of limited color change depending on lighting, temperature, the season, and its mood. It is often called the rainbow lizard because of its beautiful coloration, which intensifies during courtship and territorial displays. Common agamas are usually found in small colonies led by one dominant male, easily distinguished by its red head. These colonies are usually located in rocky areas, where the lizards spend most of their time basking and hunting for insects, small vertebrates, and plants. Some tribes in Africa use the head of the common agama to make love potions.

Size: 9 to 12 inches (23 to 30 cm)

Range: Central Africa

Habitat: Grasslands

Life Cycle: Egg-laying; three to twelve eggs per clutch, one to two clutches laid throughout year

COMMON CHAMELEON / *Chamaeleo chameleon*

Size: 8 to 11 inches (20 to 27 cm)

Range: North African coast, southern Spain, Canary Islands, Crete

Habitat: Dry, grassy and shrubby regions

Life Cycle: Egg-laying

The common chameleon is best known for its ability to change color, depending on its emotional state, the temperature, and the amount of sunlight. The lizard has two opposable sets of digits on each limb, which it uses to grasp branches as it slowly moves through the shrubs where it spends the majority of its time, only coming to the ground to lay its eggs. It can move its bulbous eyes independently to look in opposite directions at the same time. An arboreal forager, the common chameleon can extend its sticky tongue almost the length of its body to catch unsuspecting prey.

KOMODO DRAGON / *Varanus komodoensis*

Size: 71 to 94.5 inches (180 to 240 cm)

Range: Indonesian islands Komodo, Rinca, Padar, West Flores

Habitat: Grassy areas with scattered bushes and trees

Life Cycle: Egg-laying; twelve to thirty eggs laid August to October

This "land crocodile," as the species is referred to by the natives of the islands where it lives, is the largest lizard in the world. There are records of Komodo dragons longer than eleven feet (3.5 m) and heavier than three hundred pounds (136 kg). They are ferocious and capable of running at high speeds for short bursts. Many people consider them to be very intelligent because they will follow and watch a pregnant animal and wait until it is giving birth before moving in and devouring the young—and sometimes the mother, too. Because the adults are often cannibalistic, the young must spend most of their time in trees, where they are camouflaged with stripes and circular marks.

FRINGE-FINGERED LIZARD / *Acanthodactylus erythrurus*

Size: 7 to 9.5 inches (18 to 24 cm)

Range: Spain, Portugal, northwestern Africa

Habitat: Sandy areas with sparse, shrubby vegetation

Life Cycle: Egg-laying; three to five eggs

The fringe-fingered lizard is also called the spiny-footed lizard. Both names refer to the fringed scales on the sides of the reptile's toes, which increase the surface area of its feet, allowing it to run across and burrow into the loose sand. The young have bright red tails that fade to brown when they are adults. Fringe-fingered lizards are often found at the base of shrubs, where they wait in hiding for a grasshopper or other insect to walk by, grabbing the hapless prey as it struggles to gain enough traction on the loose sand to make a getaway.

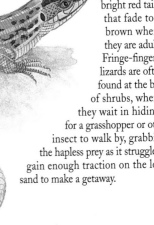
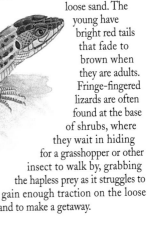

TEXAS HORNED LIZARD / *Phrynosoma cornutum*

Size: 4 to 7 inches (10 to 18 cm)

Range: Central southern United States, northern Mexico

Habitat: Arid grassy areas to desert

Life Cycle: Egg-laying; fourteen to thirty-seven eggs laid May to July

In Texas this species is better known as the horny toad, named for its rough, spiny skin and the hornlike projections on its head. A burrowing lizard, it avoids the heat of the sun by burying itself in sandy soil or hiding under rocks. It uses a defense technique displayed by just a few other reptile species: When threatened, it sometimes squirts blood from its eyes to ward off would-be predators. Unfortunately, this unique creature, once common throughout Texas, is in decline, partly because the ants on which it feeds are being wiped out through the use of insecticides.

LAND MULLET / *Egernia major*

This shiny, dark skink is the largest skink in Australia and one of the largest in the world. It gets its common name from the large scales that cover its body, which make it look vaguely like the mullet fish. The land mullet spends most of its morning basking before it goes out in search of food such as insects, small mammals, other skinks, and berries and grasses. It then typically passes the hottest part of the day hidden under logs or in burrows, emerging in the early evening to continue foraging.

Size: 20 to 24 inches (50 to 60 cm)

Range: Eastern Australia

Habitat: Variable, from grassy, rocky hills to subtropical rain forest

Life Cycle: Live-bearing; four to five young

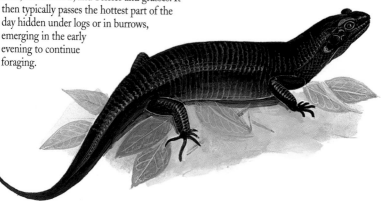

SUNGAZER / *Cordylus giganteus*

The sungazer gets its common name from its habit of resting in a position facing the sun. What it is actually doing is decreasing the bodily surface area on which the hot sun's rays may fall. The lizard has many local names that make reference to its tail—spiny-tailed, spike-tailed, club-tailed, and so on—but the most common alternate name is giant girdled lizard, which refers to the girdled or ringed scales on its tail. When it is threatened or disturbed, it runs for its burrow. Once inside, it beats its tail from side to side to discourage any potential predators from entering. Recently habitat destruction from farming and collection for the pet trade have caused its numbers to decline.

Size: 8 to 14 inches (20 to 35 cm)

Range: Southeastern South Africa

Habitat: Grasslands

Life Cycle: Live bearing; one to two young born February to March

DESERT-GRASSLAND WHIPTAIL / *Cnemidophorus uniparens*

Size: 6.5 to 9.5 inches (16.5 to 24 cm)

Range: Southwestern United States into Mexico

Habitat: Arid and semi-arid desert, scrublands, grasslands

Life Cycle: Egg-laying; one to four eggs laid May to July

Fast-moving and agile, this lizard is a member of the family Teidae, which includes many species of whiptails and race runners found throughout the New World. Whiptails are long and slender, with well-developed legs and, yes, whiplike tails. The desert-grassland whiptail is a small, lightly-striped species that eats insects. The most striking thing about this species is that it includes only females. Individuals lay eggs that hatch without fertilization. The young that emerge look like small replicas of their mother. In captivity, these lizards engage in typical courtship behavior, such as dominance fighting and displaying themselves. This is thought to trigger hormone production and synchronize ovulation and egg laying.

PUFF ADDER / *Bitis arietans*

Size: 35 to 47 inches (90 to 120 cm)

Range: Throughout Africa south of equator, Arabian peninsula

Habitat: Grasslands, semi-desert, open woodlands

Life Cycle: Live-bearing; twenty to fifty young born in late summer

The puff adder is named after its defensive display of puffing up its body with air, flattening its head, and making loud, hissing noises. A fairly common snake throughout its large range, it is known for deadly attacks: A puff adder's venom contains a potent cell-destroying component. The snake is a stealthy hunter, ambushing small mammals under the cover of darkness. Many tribal people believe that the puff adder has important medicinal value; its gall bladder and fatty deposits are thought to be a cure for many illnesses.

BIBRON'S BURROWING ASP / *Atractaspis bibronii*

Size: 16 to 20 inches (40 to 50 cm)

Range: Southern Africa

Habitat: Grasslands, semi-desert, coastal scrublands

Life Cycle: Egg-laying; seven eggs laid in summer

This burrowing venomous snake has developed an unusual technique for striking its prey and delivering venom. Most venomous snakes strike with a forward movement of the head and mouth agape. This snake strikes with a sideways motion, stabbing its prey with a hinged fang that it points out the side of its closed mouth. The adaptation—a result of living within the close confines of its burrow—makes it difficult to handle this snake safely. Holding it behind the head, normally the proper snake-handling technique, will almost certainly result in a bite. In a reference to its unusual tooth, the snake is also known as the Bibron's stiletto.

HORSESHOE SNAKE / *Coluber hippocrepis*

Size: 31.5 to 59 inches (80 to 150 cm)

Range: Southern Spain, northwestern Africa

Habitat: Grasslands, open brushy regions

Life Cycle: Egg-laying; ten eggs

This variably colored snake, with hues ranging from yellow to red to black, is easily identified by the dark horseshoelike marking on the top of its head. Its scientific name also refers to this marking: It is taken from the Greek words *hippos*, which means horse, and *krepis*, or shoe. The horseshoe snake is a diurnal reptile that actively hunts its prey of small mammals and birds, rather than waiting for them to pass near it, as some snakes do. The young feed almost entirely on lizards. When confronted by a potential predator, the horseshoe snake will flee quickly to holes among rocks or climb into shrubs.

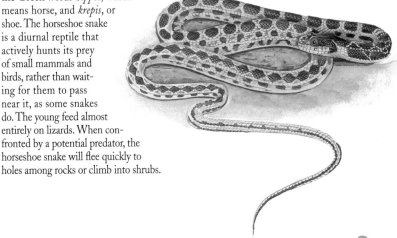

WESTERN RATTLESNAKE / *Crotalus viridis*

Size: 15 to 49 inches (37 to 125 cm)

Range: Western North America

Habitat: Wide ranging, from prairie to desert edges and open woodlands

Life Cycle: Live bearing; four to twelve young born August to October

Rattlesnakes are easily identified by the hardened segmented piece of their tail that produces a buzzing noise when shaken. Despite popular belief, the age of a rattlesnake cannot be determined by counting the number of segments in the rattle. Each time a rattlesnake sheds, it adds a new segment to its rattle. When the snake is young, it grows quickly and may shed up to four times in one year, thereby producing four rattle segments. The buzz of the rattle is part of a threat display and is usually produced before the snake strikes, although not always.

CENTRAL AMERICAN RIVER TURTLE / Dermatemys mawii

This completely aquatic turtle is the only surviving species in the family Dermatemydidae, which once was distributed worldwide. The Central American river turtle has adapted so well to life in water that it can barely hold up its head on land or support its weight on its legs. It therefore nests close to water and instead of digging a nesting chamber like other turtles, it merely makes an indent in the soil and covers the eggs with vegetation. The presence of barnacles on some specimens suggests that they enter brackish waters—unusual for most freshwater turtles. Unusual, too, is its nocturnal lifestyle. The species spends most of the day hidden underwater or floating and basking on the surface.

Size: 18 to 26 inches (45 to 65 cm)

Range: Southern Mexico to northern Guatemala

Habitat: Large rivers, lagoons, lakes

Life Cycle: Egg-laying; six to twenty eggs per clutch, two clutches laid April and December

GALAPAGOS TORTOISE / Geochelone elephantopus

These tortoises are the largest of all tortoises, with individuals weighing up to 573 pounds (260 kg). Thirteen subspecies are recognized, based on morphological features and geographic isolation. These giants were once extremely abundant, but their numbers are down to less than fifteen thousand today and a few subspecies are extinct. Early explorers, sailors, and whalers used to slaughter hundreds of Galapagos tortoises and fill their ships with live ones, since the animals would remain alive without food or water for months and thus provided a ready supply of fresh meat. Although they are now protected, their populations continue to drop due to habitat destruction and predation from feral animals.

Size: 24 to 47 inches (60 to 120 cm)

Range: Galapagos Islands

Habitat: Open grassy areas

Life Cycle: Egg-laying; two to twenty eggs

MEXICAN GIANT MUSK TURTLE / *Staurotypus triporcatus*

The Mexican giant musk turtle's Latin name *triporcatus* means "three-ridged," a reference to the three large ridges, or keels, on its carapace. The turtle belongs to the genus *Staurotypus*, which means "cross-shaped" in Greek. This alludes to the turtle's cross-shaped plastron. The same characteristic has earned the turtle an alternative common name: the cross-breasted turtle. An omnivore, it feeds on invertebrates, small vertebrates, seeds, fruits, and even mud turtles, a smaller animal. The Mexican giant musk turtle is large, highly aggressive, and capable of delivering a nasty bite. In fact, there are reports of Indian anglers abandoning ship—instead of fending off an attack—after pulling one of these turtles into their dugout canoes.

Size: 12 to 16 inches (30 to 40 cm)

Range: Southern Mexico, northern Central America

Habitat: Slow-moving waterways

Life Cycle: Egg-laying; three to six eggs

NILE CROCODILE / *Crocodylus niloticus*

Size: 138 to 189 inches (350 to 480 cm)

Range: Northern Africa (discontinuous into east and south), Madagascar

Habitat: Freshwater and brackish wetlands

Life Cycle: Egg-laying; forty to seventy eggs

These living remnants of the dinosaurs are monsters that can weigh up to 2,200 pounds (1,000 kg). They eat just about anything, including frogs, fish, insects, birds, turtles, and even large mammals. The unpredictable and ferocious Nile crocodile is responsible for more human deaths than any other African animal—more even than venomous snakes. Although it is a voracious animal, it allows other species to feed on large kills because its teeth are not designed to penetrate the tough hides of the animals it captures or to rip off pieces. The female Nile crocodile remains with the nest throughout the long (160- to 200-day) incubation period. When the young begin to hatch, they chirp, signaling to the female to dig them out.

Desert & Dry Lands

Although no two deserts are alike, one thing they all have in common is an evaporation rate greater than the level of precipitation. The result is a scarcity of water that, combined with extreme temperatures and high winds, creates sparse vegetation and a variety of adaptive characteristics among the flora and fauna that call the desert their home. Many perennial plants have no leaves or small ones, which reduces the amount of surface area vulnerable to water loss. The shallow, spreading root systems of cacti and euphorbias take advantage of light rains and absorb water quickly. The tissues of these plants are specially adapted to hold water. In addition, their thick and wax-coated stems minimize desiccation, while thorns guard the plants' store of water from thirsty animals. The resurrection plant (*Selaginella lepidophylla*) is unique in that it actually dries out and appears dead until the lightest rain revives it. Annuals cannot tolerate drought, so these plants have adapted to complete their life cycle during seasonal rains. This creates the spectacular blooms that are seen in many deserts.

Dry lands , such as the chaparral found in southern California and the eucalyptus forests of Australia, are characterized by a long, dry season with little or no rain, broken once a year by a rainy season. Despite their reduced precipitation, these areas still manage to support such vegetation as small thorny shrubs and a few scattered trees.

Amphibians and reptiles exhibit numerous adaptations to life in a realm of high temperatures and little water. Many species avoid the heat by living underground or becoming active only at night. Others, like some spadefoot toads, come above ground just to forage and breed during brief rains, while the desert tortoise emerges from its underground home to take advantage of seasonal precipitation and abundance of fresh food. Still other species, such as certain snakes and lizards, are able to remain active during the heat of the day by finding refuge in the cooler and moister microhabitats that occur in rock crevices or in the biome's sparse vegetation.

From the cacti's shallow root system that takes advantage of light rains to the nocturnal habits of many animals, the dry conditions and high heat in deserts and dry lands give rise to many specialized adaptations.

DESERT SLENDER SALAMANDER / *Batrachoseps aridus*

Size: 2 to 4 inches (6 to 10 cm)

Range: Isolated in Hidden Palm Canyon, Riverside County, California

Habitat: Water seepages in limestone rocks

Life Cycle: Unknown

One of the rarest salamanders in the world, the desert slender has an extremely limited range, living under large rocks in the seepages from canyon walls. The habitat surrounding these seepages is desert. Scientists believe that fully metamorphosed miniature adults emerge from the eggs of this species because there is very little water for a gilled larval stage. Because this salamander is extremely vulnerable to disturbance, very little natural history and ecological data has been gathered. It has been listed as endangered at both the state and federal levels, which affords it some protection. In addition, its native area has been set aside as an ecological reserve and special permits must be obtained to enter it.

MEXICAN BURROWING TOAD / *Rhinophrynus dorsalis*

With near-black skin that shows off a reddish stripe down its back, the Mexican burrowing toad is easy to identify. It is usually seen after rains, when it emerges from the burrow that it has dug with the unusual tubercles on its hind feet. If the rain leaves behind large puddles, the males start calling, often inflating their body and floating in the puddles at the same time. By inflating themselves in body this way, the toads can also fool predators into thinking that they pose a threat or be hard to swallow. In Spanish this species is commonly called *sapo barracho*, or "drunken toad," a reference to the toad's strange habit of walking backward.

Size: 2 to 3.5 inches (5 to 9 cm)

Range: Southern United States to Costa Rica

Habitat: Desert scrub, grasslands, savanna

Life Cycle: Egg-laying; two thousand to eight thousand eggs laid during rainy periods

WATER-HOLDING FROG / *Cyclorana platycephala*

When water supplies begin to dwindle, this species starts storing water in its urinary bladder and lymph system, which can later be reabsorbed into the body as the frog waits out the drought. During dry spells, it burrows into the soil with its webbed feet and sheds the outer layers of its skin, which acts as a cocoon that helps reduce water loss. Before estivation, this frog appears to be bloated because more than 50 percent of its body weight is stored water. When the rains return, these frogs emerge to drink, feed, and breed—in groups so large that they have, in at least one case, shut down a railway line because so many frogs were squashed on the rails that trains could not move.

Size: 1.6 to 2.8 inches (4 to 7 cm)

Range: Isolated areas in northern, western and eastern Australia

Habitat: Grassy areas and near temporary pools

Life Cycle: Egg-laying; one thousand to two thousand eggs laid after heavy rains

THORNY DEVIL / *Moloch horridus*

Size: 3 to 6 inches (8 to 15 cm)

Range: Inland southern Australia

Habitat: Sand and sandy loam soil

Life Cycle: Egg-laying; three to ten eggs laid November to December

The thorny devil's impressively spiked skin looks intimidating, but it isn't an armorlike barrier against predators. When threatened, the animal uses the large thorny appendage on the back of its neck as a kind of false head, hiding its real head between its forelegs to avoid injury. This species can change color rapidly, going from a pale yellow and red when warm and active to a muted dark olive when alarmed or cold. It eats virtually nothing but ants, feeding on up to twenty-five to forty-five ants a minute. Females dig nest chambers with their hind feet. After laying their eggs, they fill in the entrances to the chambers, leaving no indication of what lies below.

INLAND BEARDED DRAGON / *Pogona vitticeps*

The bearded dragon gets its name from a spiny throat pouch that it can enlarge. The small spines covering its body afford good protection. Bearded dragons will aggressively defend their territory and are often seen sitting on stumps or termite mounds surveying their kingdom. These lizards vary in color from brown and gray to more vibrant hues. In the regions where the sands are orange, so are the bearded dragons. They are ambush hunters, eating small vertebrates and insects, and their coloration usually matches the ground where they live.

Size: 18 to 24 inches (45 to 60 cm)

Range: Interior eastern Australia

Habitat: Sandy desert

Life Cycle: Egg-laying; sixteen to thirty-five eggs laid September to March

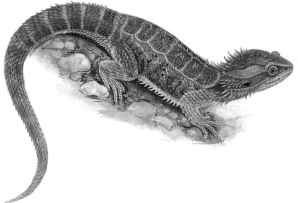

PRZEWALSKI'S SAND GECKO / *Teratoscincus przewalskii*

Size: 4 to 6 inches (10 to 15 cm)

Range: Southeastern Mongolia, northwestern China

Habitat: Sparsely vegetated cool desert

Life Cycle: Egg-laying

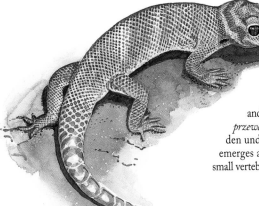

This beautiful little sand gecko has adapted to life in cool deserts, where it is active only from May to September, hibernating the rest of the year. Its beige-cream color camouflages it well against the desert sands. Most geckos have highly specialized toes for climbing on vertical surfaces, but sand geckos' feet have long thin toes with comblike projections, which increase the surface area of the foot for better support on loose sand and improved digging ability. *T. przewalskii* spends most of the day hidden under rocks or in the sand and emerges at night to eat invertebrates, small vertebrates, and berries.

AFRICAN SAND-DIVING LIZARD / *Meroles anchietae*

The desert where the African sand-diving lizard lives is regularly hotter than 122 degrees Fahrenheit (50°C), so this creature has developed some interesting tactics for dealing with heat. One solution is to hide below ground level, where it is much cooler. But because the lizard needs to hunt insects on the surface, it has perfected a behavior known as the thermal dance, which consists of raising one fore foot and the opposite hind foot. When the ones on the ground start to heat up, it changes feet. The African sand-diving lizard is also called the shovel-snouted lizard because it sports a wedge-shaped snout with a sharp cutting edge that helps it to burrow into the sand.

Size: 4 to 5 inches (10 to 12 cm)

Range: Southwestern Africa

Habitat: Sparsely vegetated sandy desert

Life Cycle: Egg-laying; one to two large eggs laid throughout year, usually December to March

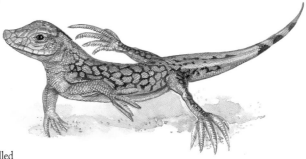

DESERT NIGHT LIZARD / *Xantusia vigilis*

Size: 3.5 to 5 inches (9 to 13 cm)

Range: Southwestern United States, Baja peninsula

Habitat: Desert scrublands

Life Cycle: Live-bearing; one to three young born September to October

A diurnal species, the desert night lizard is—true to its name—often still active after dusk. Scientists once thought that the species was rare, but research into its behavior turned up evidence that it is actually quite common. The lizard spends most of its time under leaves and debris around the base of Joshua trees, yuccas, and agaves, where it hunts for termites, ants, and beetles. The plants that it has chosen to live among are its best defense from predators. The leaves and stalks have sharp cutting edges and extremely pointed and hardened leaf tips.

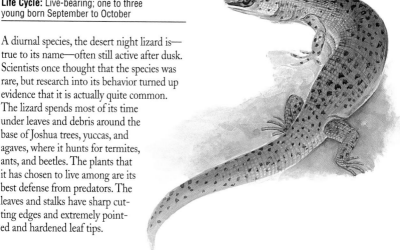

OCELLATED SPINY-TAILED LIZARD / *Uromastyx ocellatus*

The ocellated spiny-tailed lizard gets its name from the circular patterns on its body (ocelli) and its thick, spiny tail. The animal is capable of absorbing water from damp sand by capillary action through its skin. Primarily a vegetarian, the lizard can also obtain water from the plants it eats. Its teeth and jaws are specially designed to help it crush seeds and vegetation. When threatened, it will inflate its body to appear larger and harder to swallow. If it has time, it will run for its burrow and inflate its body, blocking the tunnel and presenting only its spiny tail to an attacker.

Size: 10 to 13 inches (25 to 33 cm)

Range: Southwestern Asia, northeastern Africa

Habitat: Sparsely vegetated sandy desert regions

Life Cycle: Egg-laying

TWO-LEGGED WORM LIZARD / *Bipes biporus*

Size: 7 to 9.5 inches (17 to 24 cm)

Range: Baja peninsula

Habitat: Arid regions

Life Cycle: Egg-laying; one to four eggs laid June to July

This odd-looking creature resembles an earthworm with a pair of sharply clawed, molelike front legs, which is why it is sometimes called a mole lizard. Locally, it is also

known as *lagartijas con orejas*, the "little lizard with big ears", a name referring to the stout front legs, which are located very close to the head. This digging creature is not a true lizard; it is an amphisbaenid. Most amphisbaenia have no legs at all, and this species belongs in the only group, Bipedidae, that has forelimbs. It moves through the soil by pushing with its reinforced head and scraping with its tiny limbs. The two-legged worm lizard is rarely seen, preferring to hide in leaf litter, underground, or occasionally in termite mounds.

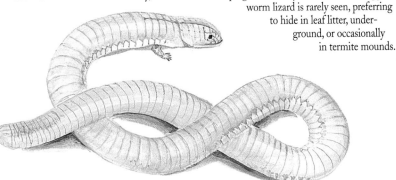

GOULD'S MONITOR / *Varanus gouldii*

One of the most common monitors in Australia, *V. gouldii* is a large lizard that forages over a wide range, at times covering more than a mile per day, eating mostly small mammals and lizards. The Gould's monitor lives underground and will often take over rabbit burrows or construct a burrow of its own. Females excavate nests in the sandy banks of creek beds or occasionally use termite mounds. The termites protect the eggs from predation, while the mound supplies them with a warm, humid environment in which to develop. The Gould's monitor will run on two legs after it has picked up sufficient speed. When cornered, it will turn and rear up on its hindlegs to seem larger, using its tail as counterbalance.

Size: 35 to 47 inches (90 to 120 cm)

Range: Australia

Habitat: Semi-arid areas

Life Cycle: Egg-laying; six to thirteen eggs

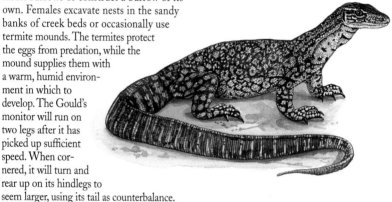

GILA MONSTER / *Heloderma suspectum*

Size: 16.5 to 22 inches (42 to 56 cm)

Range: Southwestern United States, northern Mexico

Habitat: Desert scrub

Life Cycle: Egg-laying; two to twelve eggs laid July to August

The striking reticulated patterning in contrasting colors warns its predators that the gila monster is dangerous. Indeed, it is one of only two venomous lizards in the world. Gila monsters spend almost all of their time underground, venturing out of their subterranean lairs to hunt for nestlings or young rodents, rabbits, and birds and eggs. They often hide in the shade of shrubs, where their dappled coloration serves as effective camouflage. When a threat approaches, the gila monster prefers to retreat to a burrow. But if cornered, it will bite to protect itself. Most of the documented bites to humans by gila monsters have been the result of people trying to handle them, rather than unprovoked attacks.

WESTERN SCALYFOOT / *Pygopus nigriceps*

Size: 7 to 8 inches (18 to 20 cm)

Range: Most of Australia

Habitat: Arid regions

Life Cycle: Egg-laying; two eggs

Often called a snake lizard for its snakelike appearance, the western scalyfoot has no front limbs and moves by a series of lateral undulations. Its common name comes from its rear feet, which look more like flattened, flaplike scaly projections. Taking advantage of the cool temperatures at night, the western scalyfoot forages among low vegetation, eating mostly scorpions. During the day it can be found under woody debris and other such shelters where the microclimate is less adverse. Despite its snakelike characteristics, the western scalyfoot is easily distinguished as a lizard by its external ear openings and lizard-shaped head.

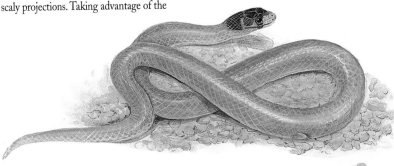

PERINGUEY'S ADDER / *Bitis peringueyi*

Also called the dwarf puff adder, this small venomous snake has evolved many adaptations to living in the desert. Its eyes are on the top of its head, enabling it to burrow underground and still remain on the lookout for predators and prey. While buried in the sand, it may poke its tail out and wiggle it in hopes of luring one of the African sand-diving lizards. These lizards provide the Peringuey's adder with most of its water supply. Occasional heavy fogs bring the adder to the surface, where it flattens itself out to increase its surface area on which the fine mist can collect. It then sucks the water off its body.

Size: 7 to 11 inches (18 to 28 cm)

Range: Namib Desert

Habitat: Sandy desert

Life Cycle: Live bearing; four to ten young born February to March

ROSY BOA / *Lichanura trivirgata*

Size: 24 to 39 inches (60 to 100 cm)

Range: Southwestern United States, northern Mexico

Habitat: Rocky canyons and desert plains

Life Cycle: Live-bearing; three to ten young born October to November

Although the family Boidae includes the world's largest snakes, the two boas that are found in the United States—the rosy boa and the rubber boa—are relatively small. The rosy boa is named after one of its color phases. It is usually found close to rocky outcrops, where it hides and hunts under rocks, in cracks, or in small mammal burrows. Being a boa, it kills its prey of small mammals and birds by constricting them before it eats them. The rosy boa does not have the typical heat-sensitive pits common to most boas. Scientists suggest that this may be because it spends much of its time probing nooks and crannies where such pits would serve no useful purpose.

JAVELIN SAND BOA / *Eryx jaculus*

Size: 14 to 27.5 inches (35 to 70 cm)

Range: Northern Africa, eastern Europe, southwestern Asia

Habitat: Desert and savanna

Life Cycle: Live-bearing, five to twelve young born August to September

The sand boa is fossorial, meaning it digs in the ground; it emerges only in the evening and at night. This secretive snake has suffered a decline in numbers throughout much of its range and is now protected in many areas. Its very small eyes are located toward the top of its head. This allows the snake to lie in wait for prey with just its eyes and nose protruding from the ground. When a small mammal, lizard, or insect comes close, the sand boa bursts out of its hiding place and grabs its prey. Sand boas, like other boas, kill their prey by constriction. The javelin sand boa is also known as the European sand boa and the spotted sand boa.

SIDEWINDER / *Crotalus cerastes*

The sidewinder gets its name from its unusual method of locomotion, which leaves telltale J-shaped tracks in the sand. Instead of slithering along in a forward direction like most snakes, the sidewinder moves sideways. This method of transport is extremely useful on the hot, loose sands in its habitat. Since sidewinding is a fast form of movement and only a small part of the snake is in contact with the scorching sand at any one time, the amount of heat absorbed while out in the open is minimized. The sidewinder is also called the horned rattlesnake because it has small scaly projections over each eye.

Size: 20 to 27.5 inches (50 to 70 cm)

Range: Southwestern North America

Habitat: Sandy desert

Life Cycle: Live-bearing; seven to eighteen young

LONG-NOSED SNAKE / *Rhinocheilus lecontei*

Size: 24 to 41 inches (60 to 104 cm)

Range: Southwest and south-central United States into Mexico

Habitat: Dry gravely soils

Life Cycle: Egg-laying; four to nine eggs laid June to August

This snake uses its tapered snout to help it dig into the ground. During the day, it hides under rocks or in burrows to escape the heat, emerging at night to hunt for small lizards and rodents. When threatened, the long-nosed snake employs an unusual defense: It coils up, hiding its head in the middle, and then begins writhing around while discharging blood from its nostrils and cloaca. Some researchers have speculated that the blood tastes bad and repels the attacking animal. The snake's tricolored pattern is vaguely reminiscent of the venomous coral snake and this mimicry may provide further protection from predators.

WESTERN BLIND SNAKE / *Leptotyphlops humilis*

Also known as a worm snake for its resemblance to an earthworm, the western blind snake is found only in areas with loose soil that permits its burrowing lifestyle. The tip of its tale features a spine that the snake uses to stick into the ground to provide traction as it burrows. The spine also acts as a defense mechanism and the sharp prick it delivers may feel like a sting or bite, which has led many people to believe erroneously that this species has a venomous stinging tail. The snake has another defensive technique: It secretes a fluid from its cloaca that contains chemicals which repel ants and termites.

Size: 7 to 16 inches (17 to 40 cm)

Range: Southwestern United States, northern Mexico

Habitat: Desert and scrublands

Life Cycle: Egg-laying: two to six eggs laid July to August

SONORAN WHIPSNAKE / *Masticophis bilineatus*

Size: 24 to 67 inches (60 to 170 cm)

Range: Southwestern United States, northern Mexico

Habitat: Semi-arid desert regions to savanna

Life Cycle: Egg-laying; six to thirteen eggs laid June to July

Most snakes are ambush hunters but the Sonoran whipsnake actively pursues its prey. And for good reason: The whipsnakes are the fastest snakes in North America. This species readily takes to the trees, where it will stretch from branch to branch in search of nestling birds and small lizards. *M. bilineatus* is active only in hot weather, typically from May to October. During the cool winters, it hibernates. The common name whipsnake was also given to a close relative of the Sonoran whipsnake, the coachwhip (*M. flagellum*). According to one myth, the large coachwhip would chase after people and tie them up to a tree by looping its coils around them before whipping them with its tail.

WOMA / *Aspidites ramsayii*

Although the woma is a python, it doesn't have the normal characteristics associated with such snakes. Instead of a broad, triangular head, the woma has a narrow head. It also has no heat-sensing pits. This latter trait may explain why almost 50 percent of the woma's diet is made up of cold-blooded reptiles, while the other half consists of warm-blooded mammals and the occasional bird. Two species in the genus *Aspidites* are native to Australia: the woma, which has a light-colored head, and the black-headed python

Size: 51 to 83 inches (130 to 210 cm)

Range: Western and inland Australia

Habitat: Desert areas

Life Cycle: Egg-laying; five to eighteen eggs laid September to October

(*A. melanocephalus*). Some researches believe that the two may actually be subspecies rather than separate species.

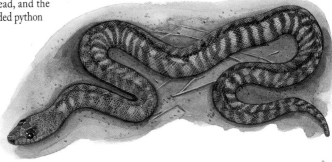

DESERT TORTOISE / *Gopherus agassizii*

Size: 8 to 14 inches (20 to 36 cm)

Range: Southwestern United States into Mexico

Habitat: Desert with sandy, gravely soils

Life Cycle: Egg-laying; two to fourteen eggs per clutch, one to three clutches laid May to July

The Latin name *Gopherus* is well-chosen: These turtles make gopherlike burrows. A single tortoise will usually have many burrows within its home range: some shallow ones for day- or nighttime rests, as well as some deeper ones to hibernate in during the winter. During the mating season, the males engage in "jousting" matches, ramming each other in an attempt to flip the opponent over and remove him as a competitor for the female. Tortoises from this genus have been declining since the late 1970s. Habitat loss has been a contributing factor, but the majority appear to have died from an upper respiratory tract disease.

Oceans & Shores

Covering two thirds of the planet, the world's oceans abound with animal life—from minnows to whales, manatees to shrimp. While amphibians are all but absent from this teeming habitat, a significant number of reptiles have adapted to

The high salt content of ocean water prohibits amphibians—with their permeable skin used for breathing—from living in the sea. Reptiles are better suited to this environment, although most marine species spend at least some time on land.

CUTTING OUT THE SALT

With thick scaly skin that is far less permeable, reptiles are better able to tolerate saltwater conditions. However, even reptile skin absorbs much more salt than needed. In response, these animals have developed a variety of techniques for ridding their body of the excess in the form of brine, a saltwater solution. Sea snakes have specialized salivary glands that excrete brine. Sea turtles have a modified tear gland that serves the same purpose, while the tongues of saltwater crocodiles are dotted with similar-acting small glands. For its part, the marine iguana has a specialized nasal gland from which it sneezes out brine when it returns to land to bask in the sun. Sea snakes are also capable of absorbing oxygen from the water. This allows them to spend far longer periods below the surface than other marine reptiles. And when they dive to great depths, they excrete nitrogen through their skin, thereby avoiding the greatest threat to human deep-sea divers: the bends.

life in the sea, notably a variety of snakes, turtles, and crocodiles, along with the marine iguana, which spends short periods in the ocean to feed on seaweed.

One of the greatest challenges to surviving in the ocean is maintaining the proper balance of salt and water in the body. This is a problem amphibians are not equipped to face. With their moist, semi-permeable skin, needed for breathing, amphibians absorb too much salt from the water to survive. Although some eighty species of frogs and salamanders occur in brackish (semi-salty) water, only the crab-eating frog of Southeast Asia is able to sufficiently control its body fluid concentrations to immerse itself in saltwater.

Other evolutionary traits that favor life in the sea are more obvious, such as the webbed toes or flippers some species have for swimming. In sea snakes, the tail is flattened laterally while the front part of the body is much thinner. This allows them to use their tail much like an oar when swimming and provides the extra mass they need to hold themselves in position when striking at prey while suspended in the water.

MARINE IGUANA / *Amblyrhynchus cristatus*

Size: 35 to 53 inches (90 to 135 cm)

Range: Galapagos Islands

Habitat: Oceans and rocky shore

Life Cycle: Egg-laying; one to four eggs laid January to February

Darwin's theory of survival of the fittest—or natural selection—is well demonstrated by this species, which is native to the Galapagos Islands. With few food resources available on the islands, marine iguanas have evolved a strategy unique among lizards: They forage in the water. The iguana's snout is short to enable it to scrape algae from submerged rocks with its teeth. On land, the species can often be found in large numbers along the rocky shores, basking in order to raise their body temperature before returning to the cold waters of the ocean. The coloration of marine iguanas is highly variable.

BLACK-BANDED SEA KRAIT / *Laticauda laticaudata*

This brilliantly banded yellow and black snake is part of the venomous family Elapidae. The subfamily Hydrophiinae is completely aquatic, while the Laticaudinae, to which the black-banded sea krait belongs, comprises terrestrial egg layers. Little is known about most sea snakes since their ocean habitat makes them difficult to study. However, this species is often seen in water close to rocky shores and river mouths feeding on eels. They are sometimes caught in great numbers when they leave the sea to lay their eggs. Their skin is sold for leather, their internal organs are used in folk medicine, and their flesh is smoked and considered a delicacy.

Size: 30 to 43 inches (75 to 110 cm)

Range: Japan to Australia, Bay of Bengal

Habitat: Oceans and shore

Life Cycle: Egg-laying

YELLOW-BELLIED SEA SNAKE / *Pelamis platurus*

The yellow-bellied sea snake—most widely distributed of all sea snakes—is commonly found drifting with the current. Its coloration provides excellent camouflage. From above, the snake's dark back blends in with the deep blue of the sea; from below, its light underside is difficult to see against the brightness of the sky. It also sometimes floats on mats of vegetation and feeds on the small fish that take refuge below. The belly scales used for terrestrial locomotion by other snakes are reduced in this species to create less drag while swimming. Because it can give birth to fully-formed young in the sea, this snake can live its entire life in the water.

Size: 24 to 43 inches (60 to 110 cm)

Range: Eastern coast of Africa to western coast of tropical America

Habitat: Open sea

Life Cycle: Live-bearing

DIAMONDBACK TERRAPIN / *Malaclemys terrapin*

The meat of the diamondback terrapin is considered to be the best-tasting of any turtle. During the late 1800s and early 1900s, food markets in large North American cities sold huge numbers for the patrons of gourmet restaurants. The high rate of exploitation of adult turtles, coupled with a low reproductive rate and a late age at maturity, caused the species to be extirpated, or severely depleted, across its range. Unfortunately, people are still willing to pay high prices for the flesh of the diamondback terrapin. This, along with the demand for small turtles in the pet trade, is likely to cause this species to decline still further.

Size: 4 to 9 inches (10 to 23 cm)

Range: Atlantic and Gulf coasts of United States

Habitat: Coastal marshes, estuaries, lagoons, brackish marshes

Life Cycle: Egg-laying; four to eighteen eggs per clutch, two clutches laid April to July

GREEN SEA TURTLE / *Chelonia mydas*

With its streamlined body and large flipper-like front legs, the green sea turtle is well adapted to life in the water, where it feeds on sea grasses, marine algae, jellyfish, crustaceans, and sponges. Its name comes from the color of its belly cartilage—the main ingredient in green turtle soup. Green sea turtles often congregate in huge numbers at nesting beaches. Despite the species' protected status, it continues to be hunted ruthlessly, especially on its nesting beaches, where the adult turtles and eggs can be collected with ease. Both remain an important part of the diet for many native populations.

Size: 43 to 59 inches (110 to 150 cm)

Range: Atlantic, Pacific, Indian oceans

Habitat: Oceans and associated shore

Life Cycle: Egg-laying; 80 to 190 eggs per clutch, multiple clutches in nesting years laid March to October in northern hemisphere and October to February in southern hemisphere

LEATHERBACK SEA TURTLE / *Dermochelys coriacea*

Size: 47 to 69 inches (120 to 175 cm)

Range: Atlantic, Pacific, Indian oceans, Mediterranean Sea

Habitat: Pelagic

Life Cycle: Egg-laying; 50 to 170 eggs laid April to November in Atlantic and throughout year in Pacific

This is the only living species in the family Dermochelydidae and it is the largest living turtle, weighing up to 1,874 pounds (850 kg). There are two subspecies: the Atlantic group and the Pacific group. The latter is lighter-colored and has shorter limbs. The "shell" of this species is actually a tough leathery skin, as compared to the typical hard turtle shell. The leatherbacks' forelimbs are adapted to life in the ocean and are more like flippers, propelling the turtles thousands of miles across the oceans to return to nest at the beaches where they were born. In recent years, many dead leatherbacks have been found with plastic bags lodged in their throats. Scientists think that the omnivorous turtles may mistake the bags for one of their favorite foods: jellyfish.

RESOURCE GUIDE

*This handy reference guide includes
a thorough contact list of herpetological
and herpetocultural societies around the
world, along with a separate selection of
informative websites and useful Internet
links. A glossary of terms appears
on pages 181 to 183.*

Important Addresses

HERPETOLOGICAL/ HERPETOCULTURAL SOCIETIES

ARGENTINA
Asociaciòn Herpetològica Argentina
Dr. Jorge D. Williams
Museo de Ciencias
Naturales
Seccion de la Herpetòlogica
Casilla 745
1900 La Plata
http://www.unt.edu.ar/AHA/DEFAULT.HTM

AUSTRALIA
Australian Herpetological Society
P.O. Box R79
Royal Exchange
Sydney NSW 2000
http://www.zipworld.com.au/~ozherps/Index2.htm

Australian Capital Territory Herpetological Association (ACTHA)
P.O. Box 1335
Canberra Act 2601
http://aerg.canberra.edu.au/pub/aerg/herps/actha/actha_hm.htm

The Victorian Herpetological Society
16 Suspension Street
Ardeer Vic 3022
http://aerg.canberra.edu.au/pub/aerg/herps/socvhs.htm

Queensland Frog Society Inc.
P.O. Box 7017
East Brisbane
Queensland 4169
http://www.brisfrogs.asn.au

Links to other Australian herpetological/herpetocultural societies
http://aerg.canberra.edu.au/pub/aerg/herps/hp03.htm

AUSTRIA
Austria Herpetologische Sammlung Naturhistorisches Museum
Wien Burgring 7
Postfach 417 A 1014 Wien

BELGIUM
Belgische Verening voor Terraniumkunde en Herpetologie
Classen Hugo
A. Sterckstraat 18
B-2600 Berchem-Antwerpen
Fax: 03 540-36-99

BRAZIL
Grupo de Estudos de Quelonios do Brasil
Fundacao Biodiversitas
Rua Maria Vas de Melo 71
Bairro Dona Clara
Belo Horizonte MG
31260-110

CANADA
The Edmonton Reptile and Amphibian Society
P.O. Box 52128
8210-109 Street
Edmonton, Alberta
T6G 2T5
http://www.ualberta.ca/~rswan/ERAAS

The Ontario Herpetological Society
P.O. Box 244
Port Credit, Ontario
L5G 4L8
http://www.geocities.com/RainForest/6560/ohs1.htm

CHINA
Chinese Society for the Study of Amphibians and Reptiles
Professor Zhao Ermi
Chengdu Institute of Biology
P.O. Box 416
Chengdu Sichuan PRC

COSTA RICA
Pro Iguana Verde Foundation
Apartado 692-1007
San José, Costa Rica

CYPRUS
Herpetological Society of Cyprus
P.O. Box 2133
Paphos, Cyprus

CZECHOSLOVAKIA
Terarista
Ing. Thomas Kucera
Strednice 51
CS-277 24 Vysoka

DENMARK
Nordisk Herpetologisk Forening
Ornevej 6
4040 Jyllinge

FRANCE
Société Herpétologique de France
Université de Paris VII
Laboratoire d'Anatomie
Comparée
2 Place Jussieu
75230 Paris

GERMANY
German Society of Herpetology
DGHT-Geschäftsstelle
Postfach 1421, D-53351
Reinbach, schicke
http://www.dght.de

DATZ Verlag Eugen Ulmer
Posfach 700561
D-7000
Stuttgart 70
Societas Europae
Herpetoiogica
Ulrich Joger
Hessisches Landesmuseum
Friendensplatz 1
D-1600 Darmstadt

Society for Southeast Asian Herpetology
Gernot Vogel
Im Sand 3
D-69115 Heidelberg

HOLLAND
Dutch Society for Herpetology and Terrariumkeeping
Mr. J. ter Borg
Nieuwe Meerdijk 253
1171 NP Badhoevedorp
http://www.xs4all.nl/~lacerta

Dutch Turtle/Tortoise Society
Nederlandse Schildpaden Vereniging (NSV)
http://web.inter.nl.net/hcc/A.Steehouder

HUNGARY
Herpetological Congress of the Socialist States
Dr. O. Gy. Dely
Zoological Dept.
Baross u. 13
H-1088 Budapest

INDIA
Indian Herpetological Society
Usant
Poona-Satara Road
Poona 411 009

ISRAEL
Israel Herpetological Information Center
Amos Bouskila
Hazeva Field Study Center
86815
Mobile Post Arava

ITALY
Italian Herpetological Society
Luciano Mariotto
Via Lencavallo 57/C
Torino 10154

JAPAN
Herpetological Society of Japan
Department of Zoology
Graduate School of Science
Kyoto University
Kitashirakawa-Oiwakecho, Sakyo
Kyoto 606-8502
Tel: +81-75-753-4091
Fax: +81-75-753-4114
http://zoo.zool.kyoto-u.ac.jp/~herp

MEXICO
Comite Herpetologica Nacional
MS Zeferino Uribe-Pena
Dept. de Zoologica
Instituto de Bioiogia
UNAM
Apartado Postal 70-153
Mexico DF

M. en C. Ma. Guadalupe Gutiérrez Mayén
Universidad Autonoma de Puebla
Escuela de Biologia
Edificio 76, Ciudad Universitaria
72570 Puebla, Puebla
Tel: 22 44-96-80
Fax: 22 44-96-80
mggitrer@siu.buap.mx
http://www.prodigyweb.net.mx/amairg/pagshm2.htm

NETHERLANDS
Tiburgse Terrariumvereniging
De Heer Ton Steehouder
Theresiaplein 24
5041 BJ Tilburg

NEW ZEALAND
New Zealand Herpetological Association
J.A. West
4 Craddock St.
Avondale Auckland 7

RUSSIA
Russian Herpetological Society
Dr. Tatyana M. Sokolova
Zoological Institute
Academy of Sciences
199034 St. Petersburg

SOUTH AFRICA
Herpetological Association of Africa
Dr. J.H. vahn Wyk
Chairman
Nasionale Museum
Postbus 266
Bloemfontein 9300

SPAIN
Asociaciòn Herpetològica Española
Apartado de Correos 317
35080 Las Palmas de Gran Canaria
http://elebo.fbiolo.uv.es/zoologia/AHE

Grupo de Estudio do Los Anfiios y Reptiles Ibericos
Juan Pablo Martinez Rico
Centro Pirenaico de Biologia Experimental
Apartado 64
Jaca (Huesca)

SRI LANKA
Amphibian and Reptile Research Organization of Sri Lanka
Anslem de Silva
Faculty of Medicine
University Peradeniya

SWEDEN
Eskilstuna Terrarieforening
c/o Mats Olsson
Rosstorpsvagan 34
633 53 Eskilstuna
016-13 14 123

Stockholm Herpetological Society
Stockholm Herpetologiska Förening
Box 38230, SE-100 64
Stockholm
Tel: +46 294 411 13
herp@algonet.se
http://www.algonet.se/~herp/

SWITZERLAND
Koorinationsstelle Fur Amphibien Und RepblienschutzIn Der Schweiz
Dr. Kurt Grossenbacher
Naturhistorisches Museum
Bermaastrasse 15
Zurich CH-8044

UNITED KINGDOM
Tortoise Trust
BM Tortoise
London WC1N 3XX
http://www.tortoisetrust.org/

British Chelonia Group
Paul Burgess
Tel: 01203 311742
bcgmailboxtwo@rmplc.co.uk
http://atschool.eduweb.co.uk/bcgonweb/index.html

British Herpetological Society
Zoological Society of London
Regents Park
London NW1 4RY
http://www.open.ac.uk/O/Academic/Biology/J_Baker/BHS.html

International Herpetological Society
A.J. Mobbs
65 Broadstone Ave
Walsall
West Midlands WS3 1JA

Scottish Herpetological Society
Bill Crowe
2 New Houses
Garvald
East Lothian EH41 4LN

UNITED STATES OF AMERICA
American Society of Ichthyologists and Herpetologists
Robert Karl Johnson
Secretary
Grice Marine Laboratory
University of Charleston
205 Fort Johnson Road
Charleston SC 29412
http://www.utexas.edu/depts/asih/
johnson@cofc.edu
Tel: 843-406-4017
Fax: 843-406-4001

Arizona Herpetological Association
P.O. Box 64531
Phoenix AZ 85082-4531
Tel: 480-894-1625
info@arizonaherpetological.com
http://www.arizonaherpetological.com/

Association of Reptile and Amphibian Veterinarians
Wilbur Amand, VMD
P.O. Box 605
Chester Heights PA 19017
Tel: 610-358-9530
Fax: 610-892-4813
http://www.arav.org/sbscrpinfo.html

The Bay Area Amphibian and Reptile Society
Palo Alto Junior Museum
1451 Middlefield Road
Palo Alto CA 94301
Tel: 408-450-0759
http://www.echo.com/~baars/

The Blue Ridge Herpetological Society
P.O. Box 727
Brookneal VA 24258
http://www.geocities.com/RainForest/Vines/5414/index.html

The Center for North American Amphibians and Reptiles
Joseph T. Collins
Director CNAAR
1502 Medinah Circle
Lawrence KS 66047
http://eagle.cc.ukans.edu/~cnaar/CNAAR HomePage.html

Colorado Herpetological Society
P.O. Box 150381
Lakewood CO 80215-0381
Tel: 303-905-6848
info@coloherp.org
http://coloherp.org

Gainesville Herpetological Society
P.O. Box 140353
Gainesville FL 32614-0353
gnvherpsoc@hotmail.com
http://gnv.ifas.ufl.edu/~wdc/ghs.html

Greater Cincinnati Herpetological Society
Cincinnati Natural History Museum
Research and Collections Facility
1720 Gilbert Avenue
Cincinnati OH 45202
http://www.acmepet.com/gchs

Kansas Herpetological Society
303 West 39th Street
Hays KS 67601
http://eagle.cc.ukans.edu/~cnaar/khs/khsmain.html

Manasota Herpetological Society
P.O. Box 20381
Bradenton FL 34203-0381
mdg@gte.net
http://home1.gte.net/mdg/memship.html

New York Herpetological Society
P.O. Box 1245
New York NY 10163-1245
Tel: 212-740-3580
http://www.nyhs.org

Pittsburgh Herpetological Society
c/o The Pittsburg Zoo
One Wild Place
Pittsburgh PA 15206
Tel: 412-361-0835
Fax: 412-361-2718
http://trfn.clpgh.org/phs

Southern Nevada Herpetological Society
P.O. Box 27912
Las Vegas NV 89126
Tel: 702-647-1652
http://www.mcneely.net/sn_herp

Tortoise Trust USA
PMB #292
204 North Oak Avenue
Owatonna MN 55060

VENEZUELA
Asociaciòn Venezolana de Herpetològica
Pietro Battistion
Apartado de Correo 567
Valencia 2001/A

ZIMBABWE
Herpetological Association of Africa
John R. Ellerman
University of Stellenbosch
Stellenbosch 7600
Zimbabwe

HERPETOLOGICAL/HERPETOCULTURAL WEBSITES

Australian Herpetological Directory
http://www.jcu.edu.au/school/tbiol/zoology/herp/herp2.html

Biosciences' links to general herpetology
http://cmgm.stanford.edu/~meisen/herp

General herpetological conservation and research links
http://www.flmnh.ufl.edu/arc/links.htm

Herp hot links (index of link pages)
http://www.xmission.com/~gastown/herpmed

Zoological record, amphibian links
http://www.york.biosis.org/zrdocs/zoolinfo/grp_amph.htm

Zoological record, general herpetology links
http://www.york.biosis.org/zrdocs/zoolinfo/grp_herp.htm

Zoological record, reptile links
http://www.york.biosis.org/zrdocs/zoolinfo/grp_rept.htm

HERPETOLOGICAL CONSERVATION WEBSITES

Amphibian Declines in Australia
http://www.jcu.edu.au/school/tbiol/zoology/herp/deline/decl.html

Canadian Amphibian and Reptile Conservation Network
http://www.cciw.ca/ecowatch.dapcan

Convention on the International Trade of Endangered Species
http://www.wcmc.org.uk/CITES/english/index.html

Crocodilians: Natural History and Conservation
http://crocodilian.com

Crocodile Specialist Group
http://www.flmnh.ufl.edu/natsci/herpetology/crocs.htm

The Herptox Page
http://www.cciw.ca/green-lane/herptox

North American Amphibian Monitoring Program
http://www.im.nbs.gov/amphibs.html

North American Reporting Center for Amphibian Malformations
http://www.npwrc.usgs.gov/narcam

Glossary

Advertisement call: Sound produced during the breeding season by male frogs and some other animals to attract mates or mark territory.

Amplexus: The mating embrace of most frogs and toads and some salamanders, characterized by the male clasping the female around the waist or the pectoral region with one or both pairs of limbs.

Arboreal: Inhabiting or frequenting trees.

Bask: To expose the body to the sun in order to increase body temperature.

Body temperature: The temperature inside the body of an animal.

Burrower: An animal that digs through the ground and lives a largely subterranean life.

Carnivore: An animal that eats the flesh of other animals.

Cartilaginous: Consisting or containing cartilage, a form of connective or skeletal tissue.

Chemosensation: The ability to detect and identify substances based on their chemical composition.

Chorus: Simultaneous calling of large number of male frogs of a single species.

Class: A taxonomic level that ranks below Phylum and above Order.

Cloaca: A bodily chamber where reproductive, digestive, and urinary end products are stored and discharged through an opening.

Clutch: A group of eggs laid during a single nesting or laying period.

Cold-blooded: Outdated term to describe an animal with a body temperature that changes with the temperature of surrounding environment. See also *Ectotherm*.

Constriction: The coiling of snakes around prey to subdue and kill it.

Core temperature: The body temperature of an animal, measured near the center of its body.

Courtship: A sequence of signals and interactions between male and female that precedes mating.

Cryptic: Hard to see, camouflaged.

Delayed fertilization: Fertilization that occurs some time after mating when sperm retained by female is brought into contact with eggs.

Dewlap: A flap or ring of skin, sometimes retractable, that extends from the throat of many lizard species.

Dimorphism: The existence of two distinct forms of a single species that differ in color, size, morphology, or other characteristics. Often males and females of a species differ this way.

Distress call: A sound created by an animal that is threatened by a predator or otherwise in danger. It is the only call frogs and toads produce with their mouth open.

Diurnal: Active mostly during the daytime.

Dorsal: Situated near an animal's back, such as the the section of a tortoise or turtle shell that covers the animal's back (also called carapace).

Ectotherm: An animal that relies on external heat sources to raise body temperature. Sometimes referred to as cold-blooded.

Endotherm: An animal that maintains a near-constant body temperature by producing heat inside the body through metabolism. Sometimes referred to as warm-blooded.

Energy budget: The difference between the energy an animal expends and the energy it takes in.

Epidermis: The skin's outer layer, often hard and scaly.

Estivation: A state of torpor or inactivity during periods of drought or high heat.

External fertilization: The introduction of sperm to eggs outside the female's body.

Fossorial: Animals adapted to digging in the ground or rummaging through ground litter.

Froglet: Newly-metamorphosed or juvenile frog.

Genus: A taxonomic level that ranks below Family and above Species.

Gestation: Carrying a developing embryo inside the body.

Hemipenis: One of two copulatory organs found in the males of some reptile species.

Herbivore: An animal that feeds on plant material.

Herpetology: The scientific study of reptiles and amphibians.

Hibernaculum: A sheltered place used by an animal for hibernation.

Hibernation: A state of dormancy or torpor during winter or other cold periods, characterized by a slowdown in metabolism and a lower body temperature.

Hormone: A substance secreted in the body that circulates with bodily fluids and produces a specific response far from its point of origin.

Insectivore: An animal that feeds on insects.

Internal fertilization: The introduction of sperm to eggs inside the female's body.

Jacobson's organ: Also known as vomeronasal organ. A pair of openings in the roof of the mouth that extend to the nasal cavity, where molecules collected on the tongue are analyzed.

Keratin: A strong, fibrous material that forms the basis of horns, claws, nails, and other horny epidermal tissues.

Larva: The first stage in an animal's development after it leaves the egg.

Lateral line: A series of small receptors on the skin of some aquatic animals, enabling them to sense slight currents and vibrations transmitted through the water.

Live-bearing: Giving birth to young that are past the egg stage. See also *Oviparous, Viviparous.*

Mark-recapture study: The study of animals that involves capturing specimens to mark or tag them and later recapturing them in order to carry out statistical analysis of population sizes.

Melanin: A dark brown or black pigment found in skin or hair cells.

Metabolic heat: Heat generated inside the body through the process of metabolism.

Metabolic rate: The rate at which energy is generated and expended by an animal.

Metabolism: The sum of all chemical processes that occur in the body, especially those associated with production or storage of energy.

Metamorphosis: The transformation of an animal from one life stage to another, such as from gilled larva to non-gilled adult with frogs and salamanders.

Mimicry: The adoption by one species of certain advantageous traits associated with another species, such as when a harmless species takes on the warning coloration of a poisonous species.

Molting: The action of shedding and regenerating the outer layer of skin.

Nocturnal: Active at night.

Olfactory: Relating to the sense of smell.

Omnivore: An animal that feeds on both plant and animal material.

Oviparous: Producing eggs that are nourished and hatched outside the body.

Paedomorphosis: Also known as neoteny. The retention of larval characteristics, such as gills, by otherwise mature animals.

Permeable: Having pores or openings that permit liquids or gases to pass through (usually refers to skin).

Pheromone: Chemicals excreted by an animal that trigger a behavioral response, such as sexual attraction, in another of same species.

Plastron: Also called ventral shell. The section of a tortoise or turtle shell that acts as a breast plate.

Receptive: Open and responsive, such as a female that responds positively to sexual stimulus.

Release call: A sound made by a male frog or an unresponsive female frog to repel a male frog that grasps it in amplexus.

Spermatophore: A gelatinous structure crowned by a mass of seminal fluid, or sperm cap, deposited by male salamanders during courtship and picked up by females.

Substrate: The solid material on which an animal lives.

Survival of the fittest: Basis of Charles Darwin's theory of evolution, which holds that the better that creatures adapt to their surroundings, the more likely they are to survive and pass on their genes.

Telemetry: A technique for monitoring movements of an animal with an electronic transmitter and receiver.

Tetrapod: A four-limbed vertebrate.

Thermoregulation: Regulation of body temperature—to maintain it at a near-constant level—through behavioral and/or physiological processes.

Uric acid: An organic compound found in large concentrations in reptile urine, giving it the consistency of a thick paste or even solid pellet, thus allowing reptiles to eliminate waste products, particularly nitrogen, with minimal water loss.

Venom: A poisonous fluid, produced by a variety of snakes and two lizard species, that is injected into prey or attackers through biting.

Vent: An outlet, such as the opening of the cloaca.

Viviparous: Giving birth to fully-formed young, as opposed to eggs.

Warm-blooded: Outdated term to describe an animal that maintains body temperature through metabolism. See also *Endotherm*.

Index

Text references are in plain type; illustrations in *italic*; photographs in **bold**; reptile and amphibian profiles in *italic* with asterisk (*).

The common names of reptiles and amphibians are listed under major groups.

H

habitat loss, 60, 61
habitat of individual reptiles and amphibians, 91-122, 124-145, 147-159, 161-171, 73-175
hearing, 13, 45
heating requirements, 72, 72-73
*Heleophryne rosei, 101**
Heloderma horridum, 81
Heloderma suspectum, 81, *166**
*Hemidactylus turcicus, 106**
hemipenis, 182
Hemiphractus proboscideus, 40
*Hemisus marmoratum, 149**
herbivores, 44, 182
herpetology, 8, 182
*Heterodon platirhinos, 114**
hibernaculum, 182
hibernation, 57, 182
homing, 32-33
Homopus signatus, 83
hopping, 51-52
hormones, 182
horny toad, *154**
Hyla ebraccata, 20
Hyla rosenbergi, 27
*Hyla versicolor, 105**
*Hyperolius marmoratus, 149**

I-J-K

*Ichthyophus glutinosus, 132**
iguana
  Cayman Island, 37
  common (green), 74, *136**
  desert, 57
  Fiji banded, *107**
  green, 74, *136**
  marine, 22, 30-31, 30-31, *173**
*Iguana iguana, 136**
Iguanodon, 16
insectivores, 182
Internet URLs, 177-180
intimidation tactics, 43, 43
Jacobson's organ, 12, 45, *45,* 182
jelly layer, *18*
keratin, 182
Komodo dragon, 22, *36, 153**

L

*Lacerta vivipara, 110**
*Lachesis muta, 140**
lamellae, 51
largest reptiles and amphibians, *36,* 78, 82, 83, 138

larvae, 18, 24, 25, 182
lateral lines, 13, 45, 182
*Laticauda laticaudata, 173**
leaping, 52, 52
*Leiopelma hamiltonii, 100**
Lepidochelys kempi, 30
Lepidochelys olivacea, 30, 31
*Leptodactylus pentadactylus, 124**
*Leptodeira septentrionalis, 114**
*Leptotyphlops humilis, 170**
*Lichanura trivirgata, 168**
life cycle of individual reptiles and amphibians, 91-122, 124-145, 147-159, 161-171, 173-175
life spans, 36-37
lighting requirements, 72, 73
lingual process, 46
Litoria caerulea, 66, 66, 68-69, *131**
live bearing, 182
  See also reproduction
lizards, 81
  largest, 22, *36*
  locomotion, 50, *50*
  medical uses of, 136
  record sizes, 22, *36*
  record weights, *36*
  running on water, 51, 81, 133
  tail shedding, 11, 41, 41, 107, 111
  thermal dance, 164
  See also chameleons
lizard(s)
  African sand-diving, *164**
  Anolis poecilopus, 37
  basilisk, 51, 81
  beaded, 81
  Bengal monitor, 22
  blindworm (sloworm), *111**
  blue-tongued skink, *110**
  Cayman Island iguana, 37
  chameleon (*Nahaqua* sp.), 9
  common agama, *152**
  common chameleon, 46, *152**
  common iguana (green), 74, *136**
  common Madagascar day gecko, *134**
  common tegu, *138**
  crocodile monitor, *137**
  Cuban anole, 21
  desert iguana, 57
  desert night, *164**
  desert-grassland whiptail, *155**

Fiji banded iguana, *107**
fire skink, *137**
five-lined skink, *111**
Florida worm (amphisbaenid), *108**
flying dragon, 51, 53, *134**
frilled, 43, 43, *108**
fringe-fingered, *153**
Gila monster, 81, *166**
Gould's monitor, *166**
gray burrowing (amphisbaenid), *109**
green anole, 21-22, *105**
green basilisk, *133**
green iguana, 74, *136**
helmeted chameleon, 81
inland bearded dragon, 66, *163**
Jackson's chameleon, *133**
Jesus Christ (green basilisk), *133**
Komodo dragon, 22, *36, 153**
land mullet, *154**
leopard gecko, 66
Madagascar mossy leaf-tailed gecko, 40
marbled gecko, *106**
marine iguana, 22, 30-31, 30-31, *173**
Mediterranean gecko, *106**
Monito gecko, *36*
New Caledonian crested gecko, *135**
northern alligator lizard, *109**
ocellated spiny-tailed, *165**
Przewalski's sand gecko, *163**
rainbow (common agama), *152**
regal horned, 42
sand-diving, 57
sloworm, *111**
Solomon Island prehensile-tail skink, 51
southern alligator lizard, 22
spiny-footed (fringe-fingered), *153**
spiny-tailed gecko (William's gecko), *107**
sungazer, *155**
Texas horned, *154**
Thai bow-fingered gecko, *135**
thorny devil, 49, *162**
toad-headed agamid, 49
tokay gecko, *136**
Turkish gecko (Mediterranean gecko), *106**

ST. REMY MEDIA

President: Pierre Léveillé
Vice-President, Finance: Natalie Watanabe
Managing Editor: Carolyn Jackson
Managing Art Director: Diane Denoncourt
Production Manager: Michelle Turbide
Director, Business Development:
  Christopher Jackson
Senior Editor: Pierre Home-Douglas
Art Director: Robert Paquet
Associate Editor: Ned Meredith
Writers: Jacquie Charlton, Brent Matsuda,
  Alan Morantz, Jennifer Ormston,
  Jessie Pratt, Thea Pratt, David Rodrigue,
  Dan Schneider, Marc Staniszewski
Writers (Species' Profiles): Angela Cone,
  Andrew Walde
Illustrators: Stephen Aitken, Ghislain Caron,
  Monique Chaussé, Patrick Jougla,
  Rosemarie Schwab
Photo Researcher: Linda Castle
Indexer: Linda Cardella Cournoyer
Senior Editor, Production: Brian Parsons
Systems Director: Edward Renaud
Technical Support: Jean Sirois
Scanner Operator: Martin Francoeur

ACKNOWLEDGMENTS

The editors wish to thank the following:
George Constable, for his editorial contributions;
Prof. David Green, McGill University,
  Montreal, Quebec
Darlene Mullan, Safari Pet Shop,
  Brossard, Quebec
Frank Slavens, Slaveware, Seattle, WA

The following persons also assisted in the
preparation of this book:
Marc Cassini, Lorraine Doré, Dominique
Gagné, Michel Giguère, Solange Laberge,
Beth Lewis, Roberto Schulz